LIFE IN A
EIGHTEENTH C

Country
House

In memory of Will Bishop, who wrote the letters, and Mary King, who did so much work to make them accessible.

LIFE IN AN EIGHTEENTH CENTURY

Country House

LETTERS FROM THE GROVE

PETER & CAROLYN HAMMOND

AMBERLEY

Illustration Note

The vignettes between each letter are from wood engravings by Thomas Bewick, except for the small picture of the Grove, which comes from an almanac of 1812, and the 1884 drawing of the gates by Thomas Garratt.

This edition first published 2012

Amberley Publishing
The Hill, Stroud
Gloucestershire, GL5 4EP

www.amberleybooks.com

British Library Cataloguing in Publication Data.
A catalogue record for this book is available from the British Library.

ISBN 978 1 4456 0865 5

Typesetting and origination byAmberley Publishing
Printed in Great Britain

Contents

Preface   6

1. The Letters   8

2. The Life of Humphrey Morice   90

3. The Grove Estate from the Beginning to 1775   111

4. The Estate Bought by Humphrey Morice   113

5. The Grove Estate from 1785 to the End   117

Appendix 1. Morice's Associates & Friends   122

Appendix 2. The Morice Portraits   126

Appendix 3. The Animals & Their Health & Treatment   128

Appendix 4. Will of Humphrey Morice   129

Appendix 5. Genealogical Tables   147

Notes   149

Select Bibliography   153

Acknowledgements   154

Index   155

Preface

This book gives a picture of life at the Grove, a large eighteenth-century house and estate in Chiswick, from the point of view of the staff. The letters at the centre of the book were sent to Humphrey Morice, the owner of the estate, by Will Bishop, his head groom, while Morice was abroad for his health. The letters were written between 1783 and 1785 (when Morice died) and describe the varied and sometimes exciting incidents in the life of the servants looking after the house and lands. There was an attempted burglary by armed robbers, the arrival of parish officers from another parish trying to enforce the eighteenth-century version of a paternity order, and the interactions between the servants. A large part of each letter is concerned with the health of the old horses and dogs whom Morice had sent to the estate to live out their natural lives in peace and comfort. Morice was very concerned with these and from a codicil to his will was aware that he was laughed at for this.

Will Bishop wrote to his master regularly, or as occasion demanded, usually about once a month. Unfortunately we do not have Morice's letters in reply, only his notes written on the letters about drafts he has sent to pay the bills that Bishop has told him about.

The book also includes a detailed biography of Humphrey Morice, with an appendix about his portraits, and a complete transcript of his will, which reveals more about his character.

There is an exploration of the lives of the servants who worked for Morice, and notes on his friends and associates, and also a history of the Grove estate before, during and after Morice's ownership.

The parish of Chiswick in the late eighteenth century was still a rural area, a collection of villages, with Chiswick itself clustered around the parish church of St Nicholas and along the riverside at Chiswick Mall, Strand on the Green also along the riverbank but further west near Kew Bridge, and the village of Turnham Green in the north of the parish spread out along the main road from London to the west. John Bowack, writing about the area in his *Antiquities of Middlesex* some seventy years before Humphrey Morice moved to Chiswick, described how 'the sweet air and situation of this place drew not only a great many considerable families to settle here formerly, but induced several illustrious persons to build seats, nor has it lost its reputation now, but is honoured with the preference of several noble persons'. In the intervening years the area had not changed much; it was still a pleasant and convenient place for a gentleman's country estate, only eight miles by water and five by road to the centre of London, but retaining its rural atmosphere. This is the setting for the letters that form the core of this book

Over the centuries the house and estate have been called by various names, always including the word 'Grove'. We have chosen to call it the Grove, as this was the name in use in Humphrey Morice's time. In more modern times it became known as Grove House.

1

The Letters

Introduction

The letters are all written to Humphrey Morice from the Grove
between 10 August 1783 and 12 September 1785. There are twenty of
them, all from Will Bishop, nominally head groom at the Grove (but
in fact far more than that, see below), to his master Morice, the owner
of the estate, first at Lausanne and then at Naples. The letters were
bought for the Local Studies Collection at Chiswick Library in 1996
from an autograph dealer. He had bought them at a stamp auction and
had no further idea of their provenance. There may be other similar
letters in existence somewhere since the ones we have start nearly a
year after we would expect them to, since Morice left England for
the last time in July 1782 and the first letter we have, dated in August
1783, does not read like the first in a series but as part of a continuing
dialogue.

The letters are all annotated in Morice's hand with notes about the
drafts for money that he sent to Will Bishop and others. They evidently
found their way back to England after his death; it is interesting to

speculate how, and where they have been since. That Morice required Bishop to send a record of all the bills to him, and that he then sent back money drafts to pay them seems to show that he desired to keep everything under his control. It would have been less trouble to allow his man of business in England to release the money to Bishop. This seems particularly odd in that sometimes he sent a draft to Richard Bull, his long-term friend and associate, to pay some bills, and once to his senior servant John Allan. There is no apparent reason why Bull or Allan should pay some bills and not others.

The People in the Letters and Their Lives

The size of the staff left behind at the Grove by Morice to look after it in his absence is not easy to work out. Various people are mentioned in the letters but it is not always obvious who they were or if they were members of staff. Nor do we know the size of the staff Morice kept when he was living there. Other large houses in Chiswick in the 1801 census of similar size, although with less ground (that is Sutton Court and Moreton Hall, both not far from the Grove), had eight male and eight female staff.[1] We know that Morice took five of his staff with him to Naples because he said so in a codicil to his will made in Naples. For these five, see below.

It is possible to reconstruct the staff left at the Grove to some extent. The one we know most about is Will Bishop, who wrote the letters in a practised hand although his spelling was distinctly eccentric, and almost phonetic. He was obviously left in charge in many ways although he is described in Morice's will as 'the groom', which was not usually very high in the staff hierarchy. He was one of the liveried staff, receiving working clothes as part of their wages and thus roughly equivalent to a footman. In Bishop's case he appears to have carried out duties which the steward or perhaps the bailiff would have taken on. His remuneration of (apparently) £25 per year would certainly seem to indicate this, although wage levels varied and all we can really say is that £25 per year is a lot more than a groom would normally be paid.[2] Bishop reported on the running of the estate, events in the house and in particular the health of the animals, mainly the horses and the dogs, which the groom would certainly be responsible for. He also ordered all the supplies needed for the animals and coal for the house. Food was not needed since the staff were on board wages (see below) and had to find their own. They may have pooled their money and eaten communally; certainly some of the dramatic events in the letters took place in the kitchen. Whatever Bishop's real status he was greatly trusted by Morice, who said in his will that he was the man he intended to leave in charge of the animals after his death and that 'he is I am persuaded very honest and will not let bills be brought in for oats, straw and tares more than have really been had'. Bishop had worked in the stables at the Morice estate at Werrington, and had been at the Grove since 1780, so Morice must have known him well.[3] From the evidence we have he seems to have been very conscientious, and in his description of his efforts to buy oats and hay at the lowest possible prices he certainly bears out Morice's trust in him. He was clearly very knowledgeable in the ways of animals and their care.

There are several examples of Bishop refusing to pay a bill presented to him without referring it to Morice. He was in fact dealing with quite large sums of money, in one letter he lists expenses at the Grove from 26 July 1782, which was perhaps when Morice left the Grove to go abroad, and the total comes to just over £1,372.[4] He was frequently sent drafts of money to pay bills. He was also a very kindly man, being concerned about the staff, calling in the doctor when they were ill, and was very upset when one of the animals was ill or died. Given these qualities it seems rather odd that Morice left him nothing in his will, although perhaps he would have considered that he had left him a job for life. He could not be sure that the next owner would keep Bishop on so the omission of a legacy does not seem very generous.

However it does seem that Bishop was kept on because we do have one piece of evidence of his activities after Morice died. This is in an account kept by John Auckland, receiver for the Duke of Devonshire in Chiswick, acting here as bailiff of Sutton Court Manor for the Duke. In this account, for 1789, 'Mr Bishopp' is noted as being paid 11s 6d for horse grass, under the heading of 'joist', a term used when grazing animals on the land of someone else.[5] As it turned out Bishop's job for life did not last much longer since on 12 October 1791 he was buried in the churchyard of St Nicholas church, Chiswick, from Grove House, aged forty-eight.[6]

The largest group of staff left at the Grove were those directly under Bishop, the stable hands. He had five of these, possibly six, William Gould, John Weeden, Henry Cross (or Chroust as he apparently insisted on being called), John Hankins, Robert Carter and perhaps John Wood who is only mentioned once, as having been ill of the flux.[7] Some of them we get to know; Henry Cross was something of a ne'er-do-well who attacked the cook and who turned out to have venereal disease, for which Will sent him to the Lock Hospital.[8] Then there was John Hankins, who had been a casual member of staff but soon after he was taken on as a permanent member of staff seems to have developed an illness from which he was not expected to recover. His imminent death was forecast in every letter, but he was still alive in the last letter. John Weeden developed and recovered from what Bishop called smallpox but which was probably chicken pox, and finally there was Robert Carter who was being pursued by Greenwich parish officers for getting a girl in Greenwich pregnant. One child was then fifteen months old and the girl was pregnant with a second, also Carter's, she said.[9] The first time the officers arrived in April 1784 Bishop said Carter wasn't at home – he was apparently in Brentford – and sent a messenger to him telling him to stay away from home for a while. The supposed mother, Elizabeth Tanner, certainly had a bastard child named Sophia, born on 7 July 1784 (marked 'Q' in the Greenwich register, the mark used there for illegitimate children). In the letter reporting this to Morice is copied a message from Carter saying he hopes he will not be dismissed and promises never to do it again. A few months later Carter asked Bishop to petition Morice for an advance of his wages to pay the officers, which Morice sent. However, the officers came back again in September 1785 accompanied by the girl's father. There were now two bastard children for which they said Carter was responsible. The one born in July 1784 must have been the child Elizabeth Tanner was pregnant with when the officers came first. There is no sign in the Greenwich registers of the first child; perhaps it was born elsewhere. Carter again wrote to Morice appealing for help. We do not know if Morice would once again have come to Carter's rescue because he had not received the letter before he died.[9]

The other senior member of staff resident at the Grove who is mentioned is John Vaughan, the gardener. The gardener of an estate was important and expected to be highly skilled. We do not have any evidence of great skills being shown by Vaughan; he is mentioned as carrying out such tasks as re-potting the orange trees and being responsible for keeping the pleasure ground mowed. In fact he had not been able to keep this tidy while Morice was away, presumably because he did not have a full staff, and so Bishop used his stable men to make hay from it after the garden men had mown it.[10] Vaughan received drafts from Morice and was thus perhaps responsible for paying his own men as Bishop was for his, and at one point he was intending to pay his men from the profit made by selling walnuts and chestnuts.[11] Bishop did give 'the garden men' their 'bread beef etc.' at

Christmas as he presumably did his own men. This must have been over and above the normal board wages.[12] Bishop does account for the gardeners in some of his periodic accounts to Morice, although here perhaps he added to his letter figures given him by Vaughan.

Another person normally equivalent to the groom in the hierarchy was the porter and here we know that this was Joseph Vickers. At the Grove he seems to have been subordinate to Bishop, since Bishop sent him to London to look at some iron work to see if it belonged to the Grove.[13] The porter was the first line of defence for the house and occupied a lodge by or near the gate. He was expected to have an imposing presence. In the letters we have a prime example of his defensive duties in the episode of the attempted break-in, which Vickers successfully fought off – literally.[14] He had also been given another duty while Morice was absent, which was looking after the accounts and supply of ale and beer for the staff. When the family was in residence these would be supplied to the staff, sometimes in what we might think of as quite large quantities. Ale and beer were provided at each meal and a quart a day for male servants was not unusual. The butler would normally have been responsible for looking after the supplies of ale and beer, but while Morice was away Joseph Vickers apparently did this duty. It appeared that the staff were helping themselves to beer and ale from stocks in the house; perhaps they thought they were entitled to it under the board wages system (for this see below), which was not usually the case. Joseph Vickers had apparently calculated that the amount drunk came to a value of nearly £24. This represents quite a lot of beer/ale given that a quart of middling beer could cost 1 penny if bought in a tavern. This beer and ale was presumably bought in since we do not have any evidence that they brewed their own. The staff agreed to pay for this at the rate of one shilling per week until they had paid for the liquor drunk. The exception was Robert Carter, who said he should not be expected to pay because he did not drink ale or small beer. Evidently this was one vice he did not have.[15] Bishop does not say whether he believed him or not.

A number of other staff are mentioned but their function is not clear. A Mr Saunders appears several times. He was obviously a person of authority since he received letters directly from Morice giving him instructions, and Bishop consulted him about various matters, usually involving the buildings. Saunders was later 'determined' not to pay the poor rates until the matter was properly settled and appealed to the Land Tax Commissioners. It seems possible that he was Morice's local man of business, his land agent. He did not receive a legacy in Morice's will.

In a large household in the eighteenth century (as well as before and after this) there were many women on the staff; the ratio between men and women varied but we would expect more than the three women staff whom we know were at the Grove during the period of these letters. It may be that there were more women and that Bishop does not mention them. It seems very unlikely that Morice would take female staff to Italy and presumably he would have employed the usual number of household staff: maids of various degree for the house, chamber, laundry, dairy and scullery. Probably the most senior woman we know about was Elizabeth (or Betty) Roberts, who was apparently the cook. In the circumstances of reduced staff, perhaps she was in fact a kitchen maid. Since the stable staff at least were on board wages – meaning they were supposed to find their own food – there should have been no need for a cook, but perhaps the staff pooled their weekly allowances, as staff on board wages sometimes did, and Mrs Roberts bought the food and cooked it for them. She was old and frequently ailing, she suffered from rheumatism and had to walk with a stick, and she was treated with great consideration by Bishop. She had apparently been sleeping in a room previously occupied by John Boham, who was probably now in Naples (see below). She had complained that this room was cold and Bishop arranged for her to occupy a warmer room, which had been that of John Allan and was on the ground floor so that she did not have to walk so far up and down stairs.[16] One interesting aspect of this exchange of rooms is that the implication is that John Boham and John Allan had slept in single rooms. That Allan, who was a senior member of staff, should do so is not perhaps strange, but that Boham, who seems likely to have been a footman, should do so seems odd. Footmen would normally have shared a room with others.

Mrs Roberts apparently did not get on well with the stable lads and in the first letter Bishop writes despairingly to Morice about the friction in the kitchen. Things seem to have improved later. When she was very ill, Susan did her work for her. We know nothing about Susan apart from this, and that she was not too well herself, suffering from ague and a severe pain in her head at one time.[17] Mrs Roberts' health slowly got worse and 'on Friday the 25th of March [1785] Elizabeth Roberts was taken ill with a complaint in her bowels attended with a fever. She on Saturday grew worse & continued so until last Saturday which carried her off about a quarter after two o'clock notwithstanding every necessary assistance was given her.' Bishop arranged for her funeral and she was buried in St Nicholas churchyard, as from Grove House, on 16 April.[18] She was noted as being eighty years old. In his will Morice had left her an annuity of £30 per year. His servant Susannah Starke was also left a £30 annuity; unlike Mrs Roberts she presumably lived to enjoy it.

The third woman mentioned by Will Bishop was Jane, also given more fully as Jane Powers. She seems to have been responsible for household duties; she moved Mrs Roberts to a better room (see above) and in the last reference to her Bishop notes that 'she takes care of all the bedding, blankets &c that no moths gets in them & likewise those things in the clothes press'.[19] We assume therefore that she was on the housekeeper's staff. She might even have been the actual housekeeper. The activities described may be part of the usual spring clean, which often took place when house-owners were not present. Like many of the other servants at the Grove Jane was not always well, suffering from an inflammation of the leg, from which she quickly recovered in 1785. As Jane Powers she was left the same legacy of £30 a year as her fellow female servants.[20]

The possibility of other female staff is raised by the information in one letter that they were producing butter and apparently selling it.[21] This was perhaps being made by an unnamed dairy maid. Staff in the eighteenth century were expected to be capable of fulfilling other jobs as well as their primary one, though. This is shown by Bishop and Vickers doing jobs not within what we would think of as their primary work, e.g. acting as Steward in the case of Bishop and looking after the consumption of ale and beer in the case of Vickers. The butter could therefore have been produced by either Jane or Susan acting as dairy maid. Carrying out duties both inside and outside the house would not have been unusual.

The five English staff Morice took with him to Naples were treated well in the Naples codicil to his will. He left a complete set of mourning clothes to each of them and allowed them to continue to live in his house in Naples, in the suburb of Chiaia, until it was the proper season to return to England. We know the names of at least two of this five, the main one being Richard Deale. Richard is mentioned in every letter because Mrs Deale, who was presumably his mother, and must have lived in Chiswick although probably not at the Grove, sent her best wishes to him and he may have written to her. Richard had been Morice's valet, at least until near Morice's death, because in the original will he is left all of Morice's clothing, the traditional perk of the valet being his master's cast-off clothing. By the time Morice wrote the codicil to his will in Naples he had a new *valet-de-chambre*, who was perhaps the Giovanni Bruscogloni who was left a much bigger legacy than the other Italian servants, maybe as compensation for not receiving his dead master's clothes. Richard was highly valued by Morice; he describes him in the will, saying 'his attention and fidelity increases every day and sorry I am to say that he is the only servant I ever had who seemed sensible of good treatment and did not behave ungratefully'.[22] Morice made Richard joint-executor of matters arising from the Naples codicil, together with John Allan (see below). He also left him a great deal else in the main body of the will, including a repeater watch, although Morice got rather muddled here as to exactly which watch Richard was to receive, leaving the same one to John Claxton in the first codicil to his will. Deale was also left Morice's diamond shoe- and knee-buckles, his gold-headed canes and an annuity of £150 per year.

One other English servant with Morice whose name we know was John (or Jack) Allan. He is mentioned frequently in the letters and was obviously a senior servant of some kind. He was authorised to sign tickets allowing visitors to see around the Grove, and was sent a draft of money, albeit for a small amount, as a payment of some kind. However he was not living at the Grove, although he had done so in the past, since as already noted Jane Powers moved Elizabeth Roberts into his old room. From some references to him he apparently moved between England and Italy.[23] He must have been expected by Morice to be in Italy most of the time since he was appointed an executor under the Naples codicil of March 1784 together with Richard Deale. He was left an annuity of £100, higher than anyone except Richard Deale.

Concerning the other English servants with Morice we can only surmise who they were. We know that one John Bohm (or Boham) had lived at the Grove since, as described above, Elizabeth Roberts had been sleeping in his old room when she complained of the cold,[24] and he was left an annuity by Morice in his will, as was Richard Harris, who isn't mentioned in the letters but was also a servant. A third person mentioned is Mr Stracey (or Stacey), who apparently also moved between England and Italy since he was described as able to tell Morice of events at the Grove.[25] The Thomas Strachey who was left an annuity of £60 per year may have been this man. These three together with Allan and Deale are probably the five servants Morice took abroad.

Morice engaged six Italian staff, we do not know in what capacity or whether male or female, but it seems likely that one of them, Giovanni

Bruscoglioni, was his new *valet-de-chambre* since he was left more money than the others, perhaps in compensation for not receiving his dead master's clothing. The other Italian servants were to be given 'forty ounces' each when discharged but Bruscoglioni was given 100 ounces or 300 ducats as well as his travel expenses if he wished to return to Florence.[26]

The Grove Finances

We learn a lot from the letters about some of the expenses incurred in running a large country house in the eighteenth century, although most of what we learn is related to expenses for running the stables. Will Bishop was apparently responsible for seeing to the payment of other bills, such as the taxes: national taxes such as the land tax and the window tax, and the various local parish taxes: the poor rate, the church rate and the highways tax. These amounted to about £120 per year, sometimes more if the land tax was higher. Other minor bills such as small building repairs were paid through Bishop, Mr Saunders, perhaps Morice's local agent, Richard Bull, an old friend and associate of Morice, or Mr Kerby, perhaps Morice's solicitor but more likely his agent in London since a Mr Wilmot who is obviously a solicitor is mentioned in the letter accompanying the will. Sundry bills amounted to about £40 per year. These and other figures discussed below are summarised in the letter that Bishop sent to Morice in November 1784.[27]

The staff were on board wages, that is they were paid a sum of money to supplement their wages to enable them to buy food, which was not supplied while the household was in semi-hibernation with the owner of the house not in residence. This was generally a temporary arrangement. These amounts varied and generally women were given smaller sums than men, perhaps on the basis that they could exist on a smaller amount of food. However Morice specified in his will that all the servants at the Grove when he died should be allowed to stay on for three months and receive ten shillings and six pence weekly, plus coals and candles and 'other such articles as are usually allowed to servants when at board wages'.[28] This sometimes, but not always, included ale and beer allowances, but not apparently at the Grove, as described above. Morice did not set different rates for male and female staff, nor for degrees of seniority.

In Bishop's summary of expenses in November 1784 he gives some figures for the amounts expended on board wages for three periods between July 1782 and September 1784.[29] We do not know at what rates the wages were paid, if different amounts were given to more senior staff or if all received the ten shillings and sixpence Morice left them after his death. It is thus not possible to get any better idea for the number of staff at the Grove while Morice was absent.

It is possible to gain a little more information from the figures for wages given in the summaries. We know that Bishop's staff were paid £10 10s a year, which is high for relatively junior staff, and it is possible that Morice paid the garden men the same amount. Bishop was apparently not responsible for seeing that they were paid, since Morice sent drafts of money to John Vaughan, the gardener, for unspecified amounts which could well have been for wages, and Vaughan intended to pay some wages out of amounts raised from selling the walnut and chestnut crops in 1783, as already noted. Nevertheless in Bishop's summary of expenses from July 1782 (when Morice left the Grove) he accounts for the sums of money for the garden men, perhaps reported to him by Vaughan. In the payment summaries there are also wages noted for 'servants' (see below), the numbers of each being unspecified. The sums involved were quite high; over the fourteen months from August 1783 to September 1784 the garden men received £95 0s. If the garden men received the same as Bishop's men then this amount of money allows for about five men. This is allowing for John Vaughan to receive the same wage as Will Bishop, £25 per year. In the eleven months covered by the period 26 July 1782 to the end of July 1783, the garden men received £137 10s. By a similar calculation this gives about twelve men on the same wage. If these figures are accurate perhaps the garden staff was reduced after the first year of Morice's absence, or there are other factors that we do not know of.

Sums of money are given as wage totals for 'servants'. We do not know who is meant by 'servants'. Since Bishop seems to report his own stable men separately it probably does not include these (they are not listed in the summaries), thus it probably means at least the three women whom we know were on the staff in 1783–85, together with possibly others who Bishop does not mention. On the assumption that all of them were relatively young, a junior female servant could expect about eight pounds per year at this time and the sum of £47 14s given for the fourteen months between the beginning of August 1783 and the end of September 1784 allows for five staff at this wage. The larger sum of £64 18s in 1782–83 allows for seven servants. These figures certainly allow for more 'servants' than we know about, even adding Joseph Vickers, the porter, to the servants. At least these figures give some guide to the numbers of staff present in the period covered by the letters.[30]

Since we have figures for the expenditure on the animals and the staff looking after them in the letters it seems a worthwhile exercise to calculate the total over the most complete year, September 1783 to September 1784. The figures are necessarily approximate as it is not always clear what is the period covered by the bills. The results are as follows, rounded to the nearest pound.

Oats	£134
Hay, straw and tares	£203
Bran and raspings	£19
Dog meat	£50
Veterinary bills (Mr Richins)	£34
Veterinary bills (Mr Salter)	£10
Livery costs (stable men)	£11
Wages, including Bishop	£65
Total	£538

The total is very close to the £600 that Morice left in his will to pay every year for the expenses incurred in looking after the horses and dogs, and shows that he had calculated the amount very carefully.

The Letters Themselves

The letters are on paper of varying sizes, ranging from sheets measuring about 15 by 12 inches down to half that size. Perhaps Bishop tore larger sheets in half if he did not have a great deal to say. One letter is part of a letter torn from a half-sheet and there are also three incomplete parts of letters. These have been printed with the letters they were folded with since they were not dated. Two are with Letter 3 and one is with Letter 19. They have clearly been torn or cut from larger letters.

All the letters are folded to a size of about 5 by 3 inches and the address written on the resulting blank panel. All were sealed, mostly with a seal marked 'WB' for William Bishop, presumably applied by Bishop himself. Two are addressed to Morice at Lausanne and the rest to Naples in the form 'Monsieur, Monsieur Morice, a Naples'.

They are signed on the back fold by J. Kerby, who is mentioned occasionally in the letters and was probably Morice's man of business in London. A John Kerby of Stafford Street in Mayfair, near Morice's

London town house in Dover street, was one of the witnesses of Morice's will. The hand used to address them is firm and clear and does not look like either that of Bishop or Kerby. Perhaps it was that of a clerk in Kerby's office.

All the letters are marked 'Paid 1 shilling'. This was the cost for a one-sheet letter via Hamburg. From here they were carried on the Thurn and Taxis Imperial postal system through Europe. The letters addressed to Naples are all stamped '*Germania*', a stamp applied by the Naples postal office in Rome, with a handwritten '7' for 7 grana, the cost within Italy.[31] On the address panel of each is written in red '83', '84' or '85'. This is probably an annual filing mark added by Morice. All of the letters to Naples have notes relating to the contents, written in Morice's hand and signed 'H'. These notes are described as being on the address panel.

Editorial Procedure

The letters were all transcribed twice, firstly by two independent volunteers from the Brentford and Chiswick Local History Society (see the names listed in the Acknowledgements) and then each pair of transcripts were harmonised and checked again by the late Mary King. Mary also 'translated' each letter into modern English, although she left Bishop's idiosyncratic diction and phrasing intact, and retained his spelling of proper names. Abbreviations, of which there were many, have been extended, e.g. 'Honoured' was almost always spelt 'Honrd' with a superscript 'd'. In the interest of clarity this modernised version is the one that has been used in this book. Line breaks and punctuation have been modernised, and lists set out properly. Dates have been put into modern format and paragraphs have been inserted where appropriate. Square brackets are used for editorial notes, including noting the annotations in another hand, always that of Humphrey Morice, and also for the numbers of the notes containing additional information which are placed after each letter.

One of the letters in the original spelling is given below and there is a photograph of Letter 3 on page 103.

Honrd Sr   The Grove   12th Septbr 1785
On the 3d I receved Your Honrs letter Deated the 8th August
With the fouer Drafts - On Monday night & all Day
Tuesday we had Dreadfull Stormey weather the
Wind blew Exceeding hard at south west which has

Blown Down one of the greate Arbbale Trees in
The pleashure ground & the great Thorn tree by
Oronookos paddock & A number of limbs in the
parke - & Stript one End of the roof of the Shade in
The back yard - & broke A great number of Tiles
Which I have had repard, -
Since I wrote my last the great bay Mare gentry cammil,
Has had A Youmor fell in to one of her Hind laggs
Which was Swold very much I have given her a
Dose of physick & She is A great Deale better -
Last Monday two of the Greenwih Officers & old Tanner
Came heare to take up Robert Carter for the Expence
of the two Basterd Childern Sworn to him some time
Back by Elizabeth Tanner - but thay mist him
However thay are Detirmmind. to have him In
Case he Dose not pay Down 20 pound.
The following is what Robert Desierd me to Send You
[written above] 12th Sept 1785
Honrd Sr I bagg pardon for trobling You Again and
For what I have bin guilty off and am sorry to Empart
That adversety Obliges me to resume my former
Petition for the Greenwich Gentlemen are
Detirmened not to lett me rest in peace Except
I comply with thare request wich is quite
Inconsistant to my Abbilitv at present as I have
No more money then my present Youse requires
So in case I am taken Your Honr is senciabl what
Must insue or Marry the garle which I am
Detirmened at all Events never to Acquiesce
To am Verey thankfull for what. Your Honr have
Allredy Dun for Me and at this Critical time
It may be the Means of preventing Your unforti
nett pettioner frome utter ruen - so Rest in
Hopes to Expearance Still Your Honrs goodness
That Sr You will be pleased to Advance me
One Years wages or twenty pounds on Acct
To Settle the Affare & Your petitionr as In
Duty bound will Ever pray

I am Sr Your Honrs Servant
at Command Will Bishop

Letter One [1]

The Grove, 10th August 1783 [August is written under a deletion which seems to end in 't']

Honoured Sir

Last Tuesday we had a strange dog came into the yard, pleasure ground and park and bit several of our dogs and one of the horses, old Tack that came from Marshgate [2]. The dog was seen to bite Toper, Flippant, Snap & Cutty in the park, Captain he bit in the yard, Rattler, Phyllis, Flora & one of the young puppies he bit in the pleasure ground. He was very near the old blind carthorse Spritely but we cannot tell whether he bit him or not. I have given all those that was bit or seen to be near him the Ormskirk [3] powders. The two horses I have given them two doses each. There is no wound through the skin of any of them, the dog snapped at them as he came near them. They are all well at present and I hope there is no danger of their [not] doing well. Twister was taken yesterday with his old complaint, bound up in his body and not able to dung. I have treated him in the same manner that relieved him when he had this complaint last. On Tuesday evening Slamekin's filly was found dead in the hovel in the meadows. She was very well in the morning, feeding with the other horses. There being no signs of her having struggled where she lay I conclude that she dropped down and died in a moment.

Old Tartar is very lame by a kick he got from some of the other horses, just below the elbow on the off leg before [4]. It is very much swelled, I expect it will break in a few days and soon get well. The coach horse Silver has got a kick on his hock on the near leg behind, he is getting better.

I am sorry to acquaint Your Honour that there is scarce any bearing with the goings on between Elizabeth Roberts & the stable lads. It is not one in particular but all of them at times, they are continually a-quarrelling, she with them and they with her. The lads says that they cannot pass in the house quietly for her, that she is always abusing them, calling them blackguards & dirty fellows and such like expressions. On the other hand she says that they are always abusing her, that she cannot be at quiet for them. There was a quarrel last Friday arose between Elizabeth Roberts and Henry Cross, the new lad who came in Thom Collett's place [5], about setting on a tea kettle of water on the kitchen fire. I find by Will Gould who was present when the quarrel began that she attempted to push Henry into the fire first. Henry then had the impudence to kick her back side and struck her on the hand. Suppose she was the first that begun the quarrel. A woman of her age ought not to be treated by a young lad in that unbecoming treatment, nor any other woman in the manner she was treated. I am sensible that there has been a great animosity between her and the lads for a long time.

Stracy [6] can if he will acquaint Your Honour more of the particulars what has been the reason of all the disturbance between she and all the lads than I am able to acquaint you in writing.
I am Your Honour's Servant at Command
Will Bishop

One thing I have remarked there have never been a woman placed in the kitchen here but there has always been a something between them and the stable lads to create a disturbance in the family [7].

[on address panel] Mrs Deale is very well. Desires to be remembered to Richard [8], hopes Your Honour and all is well with Your Honour

[Written on the outside by Morice] W. Bishop, received 23th August, answered 30th, 1783

Notes

1. This letter is addressed to Morice in Lausanne.
2. This is probably the Marshgate in Cornwall, not far from Werrington.
3. Ormskirk powder was a mixture of powdered chalk and a clay mixture with several other ingredients, including oil of aniseed to make it palatable. It was given as a so-called cure to both animals and humans, although in neither case would it have had any effect. Bishop was obviously aware that the important point in this case was that none of the animals showed that the mad dog had broken the skin and so introduced the rabies virus.
4. The elbow of a horse is the joint of the front leg where it meets the belly of the horse. See also note 8 of Letter 4.
5. We know nothing further about Thom Collett.
6. Stracy was perhaps a member of Morice's staff who moved between

England and Italy. The man in this letter is probably the Thomas Strachey who was left an annuity and a legacy in the will.

7. This is the first of two references to the 'family' (the other in Letter 7), in the sense of the body of persons living in the house, not necessarily related to one another.

8. Richard is sent remembrances from Mrs Deale in every letter. He was probably her son. Morice left him very generous bequests in his will (see above pp. 14-15).

Letter Two [1]

The Grove 25th August 1783

Honoured Sir

I am happy to acquaint Your Honour that all the dogs are well and the two horses, as it is almost three weeks since they was bit I conclude that they are all out of danger. I am told that the same dog was at Brentford and bit a great number of dogs there, some have died mad and several have been destroyed which was bit at the same time as ours was bit. Twister is quite well of his complaint. Old Tartar is getting better of his lameness but it has pulled him down very much, he being so old and feeble that he will not be able to hold out much longer. He is so weak now that he cannot get up without help when he is down. Poor old Nickey breaks very fast, I don't think that he will last all the winter. Silver the coach horse is quite well of the kick. I have had the good fortune to save all the second crop of hay without any rain. I have now got hay enough to last all the old horses two years, and much better got in than any we ever had since we have been at the Grove.

On the 19th instant I received Your Honour's letter dated 2nd with the drafts &c. I am trying Junice with the calomel magnesia [2] etc.

Mr Salter advises 30 grains of Calomel [3] to be given every night for three weeks, in case it does not affect his mouth, if it should, to stop giving it until the soreness is gone off. He has taken it only three nights as yet.

I have been so busy in getting in my hay that I have not had time to make inquiry about the oats as yet. There have been a fine time here for hay making & harvest and very fine crops in general, hay and straw of course will be cheaper than it was last year.
I am Your Honour's Servant at Command
Will Bishop

Mrs Deale gives her Duty to Your Honour, is very happy to hear Your Honour is got better & desires to be remembered to Richard. She is very well at present

[Written on the outside by Morice, in red ink] W. Bishop August 1783

[Written on the back fold in Morice's hand] About hay for two years, H

[Two short letter fragments are folded in with Letter 2. The top one has an edge torn and the missing words are added conjecturally. Neither fragment contains any guide as to when they were written. See page 18 of the Introduction]

Fragment 1

[I for]got to speak to you about the ale and small beer [4] [missing] is left but I concluded that you meant that the people [ought t]o pay for it out of their board wages the same as they did when you was abroad last. The account that Joseph Vickers have given me of the ale and small beer amounts to £23.19s.9d. They have all agreed to pay a shilling per week until the money is all paid, except Robert Carter, he thinks that he has no right to pay anything towards the beer as he never drinks any ale nor small beer.
[On the reverse is written Morice, Perigeaux [er] Paris and incomplete sums in Morice's hand which do not relate to the price of the ale and beer.

Morice was perhaps at Perigeaux on his way to Nice (where he signed a codicil to his will on 10 October 1782, see below pp. 142-3) and hence to Naples via Lausanne, see Letters 1 and 2].

Fragment 2

Mr Drew the tallow chandler sent his bill and the account of the kitchen stuff. His bill is charged £11.1s.0d for candles [5], he has had 143 pound of kitchen stuff which I conclude is to be deducted from his bill.
Ann Paine of Knightsbridge has sent the bill for the ass [6] charged £9.13s.0d
[in hand of Morice] Paid by a draft.
Mr Jenkins the turner in Clifford Street [7] has sent his bill charged £5.15s.0d.
I shall not pay any bill without first having an order from Your Honour.
Charles Sloecomb set out last Monday morning to see his [8]

Notes

1. This letter is addressed to Morice in Lausanne.
2. Calomel Magnesia. These are two different remedies and it should probably read 'calomel, magnesia'. They would not normally be used together, magnesia was and is used to treat mild stomach upsets. It sounds almost as if Morice had suggested this as a cure although we do not know for what.
3. Calomel is mercurous chloride and was frequently used in medicine both human and animal. Since it is poisonous it has to be used carefully. The dose suggested by Mr Salter (one of the vets whom Bishop frequently consulted; the other was Mr Richins, also of Richmond) was not excessive but in the next letter he greatly increases the recommended dose. This would certainly cause problems, as Bishop reported, particularly in the next letter. The mouth dryness and hence a reluctance to eat are symptoms of mercury poisoning. Bishop seemed well aware of this. We do not know why the horse was being treated thus. Bishop had presumably reported the problem in an earlier letter, but it could be that Junice was being treated for the heaves (a difficulty in breathing), and from the next letter it sounds as if he thought the calomel might help the lameness.
4. Small beer was weak beer, normally drunk at meals. Joseph Vickers was a member of staff, and here responsible for looking after the ale and

beer supplies. This would normally be the responsibility of the butler but Vickers was apparently the lodge-keeper, and Bishop was not responsible for his wages [Letters 13 and 18].

5. We do not know how many candles were bought for this sum and so cannot tell if Bishop was paying less or more than others. The 'kitchen stuff' was presumably surplus vegetables produced at the Grove by Vaughan and his men.

6. Asses' milk. Chiswick Local Studies Library has a bill from Ann Paine and Co of Knightsbridge for asses' milk, half a pint per day, delivered in 1781. This was for one month's supply costing £1. 10s. 0d., which suggests that the bill of £9. 13s. 0d. was for many months. The Library has another bill dated 1781 from an Esther Lowther, also of Knightsbridge, who as well as supplying milk supplied an ass and foal for one month over Christmas. Asses' milk was said to be good for various health problems and to have unique nutritional value. Morice suffered from health problems all his life, what he described as 'the old complaint in my breast which I have been subject to ever since I was a child' as well as recurrent gout. (Letter from Naples in 1768, Centre for Buckinghamshire Studies, D/LE/D/8,19).

7. The Duke of Devonshire owned much property in Clifford Street in London, and it is possible that Mr Jenkins was a tenant of the Duke who was a near neighbour of Morice in Chiswick and that this is how Morice came to employ him.

8. It sounds as if Charles Sloecomb, also spelled Slocumb, was at this time a member of staff but from Letter 3 of 20 September he has obviously left.

Letter Three [1]

The Grove 20th September 1783

Honoured Sir

On Monday the 15th I received two letters from Your Honour, one dated the 23rd, the other the 30th of August with the drafts. The amount of the bills which I sent to Your Honour in my letter dated the 1st of August is –

Mr Wopshot's Bill [2]	£49.5s.8d
Mr Beniworth's Bill for raspings [3]	£14.5s.5d
Mr Beniworth Bill for bran	£2.17s.4d
Mrs Pulling Bill	£3.16s.0d
Mr Holmes Bill	£3.1s.0d
Mr Jullion's Bill	£3.7s.6d
Church Rates [4]	£5.16s.6d

[Written in the margin in Morice's hand]
Paid by a draft 28 Nov 1783
£2.17s.4d
£16.15s
[Total]   £19.12s.4d as on the other side   [referring to £16.15s for tradesmen's bills, see below, written on the other side of the sheet].

The amount of them are all sent except Beniworth's bill for bran and Mr Jullion's bill. As soon as I received the letter from Mr Kerby [5] which was on the 4th of this month concerning the trunk that was left behind, I carried it to town. Mr Kerby owned to me that he had orders about this trunk, and says that he thought it was sent when the other things was sent to Naples. This trunk was left in the library without a direction on it, all the other things was in the porter's hall with directions on them. After all hopes was over of sending them by sea I fetched them to the Grove. I then mentioned it to Mr Kerby about this trunk, who then said that he believed it was not to have been sent by sea as there was no direction on it. I likewise mentioned it to him again when I carried the things back to town to be shipped for Naples. He then said that he supposed it was not to go.

Mr Salter increased the Calomel [6] from 30 grains to sixty, from sixty to ninety. At the end of 17 days it seized his mouth so that he did not care to feed or drink anything. As soon as I found that it had seized his mouth, I stopped giving him the Calomel. The soreness of his mouth is not quite gone off as yet. He is much as he was in regard to his lameness.

Tartar the blind horse is quite well of his lameness but the poor creature grows very weak and feeble and so does old Nickey. I fear they won't hold it out all the winter. All the rest of the horses are much as usual.

I am sadly vexed about my poor old dog Ranger. A few days after I wrote to your Honour last he was all of a sudden seized with a convulsion fit [7] which held him about ten minutes.
When the fit was over I bled him. I consulted Mr Salter about him, he give me some pills to give him. He has continued to have two or three fits every day and much stronger and lasts on him a great deal longer than they did at first. He looks very dull about the eyes and seems to be quite stupified and he has lost his hearing and seems to have a giddiness in his head as he staggers as he walks. He eats and drinks very well when the fits are over but I am sadly afraid that one of these fits will carry him off before it is long. The rest of the dogs are all well.

It is very extraordinary of Henry Cross, the lad who quarrelled with Elizabeth Roberts, it came out one day last week that he had got the fowl disease [8] on him, and he had applied to Mr Curtis for relief without my knowing anything of it. When I spoke to him about it he said that it had not been on him above a fortnight, but Mr Curtis told me that he must have had it on him a long time, although he had not applied to him above three days before I spoke to him about it, and that the best way would be to send him to the hospital as he had it very bad on him. I having found a letter of recommendation in one of my drawers that was signed by Your Honour for the Lock Hospital [9] I sent him there last Thursday.

John Weeden have been ill with a fever & a cold for three or four days but he is got almost well again now [10].

The Clerk Mr Cotton [11] came for the Curate's Afternoon Lecture [12] and for his Christmas Box, I told him that I would acquaint Your Honour of it.

Last Wednesday the Marchioness of Rockingham [13] & two gentlemen came to see the Grove with a ticket that is wrote and signed by Mr Allan dated 26th July.

The following bill is sent in:

Frances Morgan's [14] bill for carpenter's work	£5.0s.4d
John Francis two quarterly bills	£2.16s.0d
Nicholas Taylor's bill for cooper's work	£0.19s.2d
Matthew Wright's Bill [15]	£2.6s.0d

Abraham Shermas monthly bills from the 1st
  of July 1782 up to August the 30th 1783   £3.8s.0d
John Maxwell's bill for general evening posts [16]   £2.5s.6d
                         [Total]   £16.15s.0d

We shall be sadly put to it in drawing out all our dung [t]his winter having only two cart horses, and they beginning to grow in years are not so well able to work now as they used to be some years back, so that we can only work one cart at a time. If we had two more horses they would greatly ease the two old ones and we should be able to do as much work in one day as we now can do in two days with the same number of people
I am Your Honour's Servant at Command
Will Bishop

Hiring of cart horses here is very expensive. There is no getting a cart horse under half a crown a day besides his keep and another thing is you cannot get them at any rate sometimes or when they are most wanted.

Joseph Vickers gives his duty to Your Honour. He would be glad to have a new great coat this winter, he having had his old one this six years it is quite wore out [17].

Mrs Deale gives her duty to Your Honour, is sorry to hear that you are not quite so well as you was, desires to be remembered to Richard. She is very well.

Mr Jennings have brought the clothes for us as usual but I desired him not to make any of the clothes for Henry Cross nor for the other helper [18] when he came to measure us, until I know Your Honour's pleasure whether they are to have any or not, as Henry's behaviour has been so indifferent & the other not being hired by the year.

[on the address panel Morice has written] W. Bishop found at Naples, Answered 18th November 1783, about bills. H

Notes

1. This letter is addressed to Morice in Naples, as are all subsequent letters.
2. Mr Wapshott was a member of a Chiswick family of butchers, and seems to have supplied much of the meat in the area including to the

Duke of Devonshire at Chiswick House and to Chiswick Workhouse.

3. Mr Beniworth was a baker as well as a corn merchant. He supplied 'sacrament bread' to the parish church. Raspings are small breadcrumbs in modern parlance.

4. The church rates for 1783 were set at 3*d* in the pound, thus Morice paid as noted in the letter on a house rated at £466. The parish had agreed in 1779 to rate properties at the rental value of the house and estate.

5. Mr Kerby, a man of business to Morice. He is mentioned frequently, often in connection with money drafts. See biographical notes p. 19.

6. Calomel, see notes 2 and 3 of Letter 2.

7. Fits in dogs are not uncommon. They are sometimes caused by intestinal irritation caused by a change of diet, although in this case this seems unlikely. Perhaps it was old age.

8. Fowl disease, that is venereal disease. Mr Curtis was the local doctor, always consulted by Bishop in medical matters. He had been in Chiswick since 1770 and stayed there until he died in 1805. He is described as a surgeon in *Eighteenth Century Medics* (P. J. and R. V. Wallis *et al.*, 2nd edition, 1988, p.149). Two large bills of his were paid later, see Letters 7 and 16.

9. The Lock Hospital was for the treatment of venereal diseases. It had been founded in 1746, and was near Hyde Park Corner. It seems probable that Morice was a subscriber to the hospital since he was able to recommend patients for treatment, although this was not one of those he left money to in his will. The medicines used to treat venereal diseases in the eighteenth century were not very effectual. Interestingly one of them was the mercury compound calomel, which Bishop was using to treat his horses (see above, note 6).

10. Weeden's illness was quite probably just a feverish cold and nothing more.

11. Mr Cotton was the vestry clerk. He had been in office for many years and had beautiful handwriting. He came for his Christmas box in 1784 and 1785 too, see Letters 13 and 19.

12. Curate's lecture. Parish lectures were usually sermons delivered by someone chosen by the parish, sometimes when the local clergyman was disinclined to give sermons. The lecturer was sometimes the curate, as here, but not necessarily, although he would be in orders, deacon or priest, and was licensed by the bishop. He was supported by the parish. See also Letter 13.

13. Visiting great houses was a fashionable custom; frequently a pass or ticket of some kind was needed as it was here. The Marchioness

of Rockingham was not a relation of Morice but was a fairly near neighbour, living at Uxbridge, and they may have known each other. From the references to Mr Allan he appears to be a fairly senior member of Morice's staff, usually with him in Italy; Morice refers to him at least once as Jack Allan, a familiar form of address. See p. 15.

14. This woman carpenter is mentioned several times, she (or her firm) were used regularly by Bishop.

15. The Dukes of Devonshire at Chiswick House regularly employed bricklayers named Wright, although we do not know if any of them were named Matthew. This Matthew Wright was very likely of the same family.

16. John Maxwell was presumably the local postmaster. He was paid several times for the evening posts, collecting or delivering or both, we do not know. See also Letters 13 and 19.

17. New livery clothes were apparently sometimes bought as needed rather than at regular times, as was usually the case in other great houses; for example see Letter 5, where Bishop asks for a selection of clothes for members of his staff.

18. The 'other' referred to here is probably John Hankins, who was not given permanent employment until January 1784, see Letter 6.

Letter Four

The Grove 30th October 1783 [the date is probably in Morice's hand]

Honoured Sir

I had forgot to mention in my last letter that I catched two of Chiswick men a-cutting the reeds in the lower meadow with an intent to carry away. I got a warrant and took them before Justice Lamb who give them a severe reprimand, made them discharge the warrant [1] and paid the expenses &c and quitted them on their promising never to trespass again. On Sunday the 5th instant eleven men from Mortlake got over the iron gates at the bottom of the park to steal the walnuts. We not knowing any of them, John Vaughan got a warrant on suspicion for two of them, which proved to be right as their friends appeared for them before the Bench of Justices, and promising that they should never offend again the Bench let them off on paying a fine of one pound one shilling, that is five shilling damage & five shillings to the poor of the parish & eleven shillings for expenses & discharging the warrant.

I have made all the enquiry I can about the price of oats at Kingston & other markets. I am told that the cheapest place to buy oats at is at Bear Key [2] Market in Mark Lane. I went one day to see the way of the market. I find that they are all corn factors that resorts the market for selling of corn. Most of the corn factors from Richmond, Brentford, Turnham Green &c goes to Mark Lane to buy oats, it being the best market for buying of oats at. Mr Denyer, a maltster at the Strand on the Green who keeps the market constantly twice a week, tells me that the best way of buying of oats is to take the chance of the market, not to deal always with one corn factor, where a man constantly keeps the market has a much better chance of buying of oats cheaper than a man who seldom or never goes to the market, especially if he carries ready money to market. He tells me that he buys oats for several people and they allows him sixpence per quarter for buying, that he always gets them a shilling or two cheaper in a quarter than any corn factor will send them in at by an order, as they will always charge the top of the market if their oats are not so good by two shillings the quarter as those that are sold at the top of the market. I have had two twenty five quarters of oats of Mr Marratt since he sent his bill in. The first 25 quarters he charged £1.7s.6d per quarter, the last 25 are got down to £1.3s.0d [3]. It is thought that oats will be cheaper before it is long as the new oats are much better than the old ones are.

Some time back I spoke to Mrs Chandler about the price of hay and straw for the ensuing year. She at first stood out to have the same price as last year, that is hay at £3.15s.0d per load and wheat straw at 11d per truss [4]. I told her that I had an order not to deal with her unless she would lower her price this year according to the times or at the same price as other people would contract for a year. She then said that she would lower the price of the straw a penny in a truss but would not lower the price of the hay. I made an enquiry of a farmer or two what they would contract for. For a year certain, one farmer Bowlden of Turnham Green offered the lowest price, hay at £3.12s.0d per load, and wheat straw at 9d & oat straw at 7d per truss. I sent Mrs Chandler word that I had found a person that would serve a year certain hay at £3.12s.0d and straw at 9d & 7d the truss. If that she would serve at the same price I would deal with her sooner than a stranger as she had served Your Honour so long. She sent me word that she would serve at £3.12s.0d for hay and 9d & 7d for straw as I had been offered at that price. A few days afterwards I went to Mrs Chandler to contract with her at the price she had agreed to. She then told me that she had altered her mind and would not agree unless I would give her 10d per truss for straw and the same price for hay as last year. I told her that I had given her the first offer & if she did not choose to accept of it I would not give her the price she asked, which she refused, and I have agreed with farmer Bowlden for the ensuing year. Mrs Chandler's year will be up on the 22nd of next month.

The Overseers of the poor have been for the poor rates, £34.19s.0d due at Michaelmas last. I told them that I would acquaint Your Honour of it & that there had been a hearing at the Vestry concerning the poor rates [5]. As soon as it was settled they would be paid.

Mr Weatherstone [6] who made so much disturbance in the parish died suddenly in a few days after the Vestry was over.

Junice mouth – after the soreness was quite gone off I repeated the calomel [7] again. In three days it had the same effect as before. He is much as usual with regard to his lameness. Poor old Tartar is gone off at last [8]. After eating his corn in the morning and appeared to be as well as he had been for some time past, in less than an hour afterwards he dropped down and died in a few minutes just by the edge of the pond where he had been drinking.

The bay mare Jenny Cammile & the brown horse Little John have both got a dry cough on them, they have always had a cough on them at times ever since they had the strangles [9], much the same cough as your mare have had on her so long, but now they are a great deal worse than they used to be. Notwithstanding Mary Denford has had a dry cough on her so long, she is no worse now than she was three or four years ago. I am trying the commin cordial balls [10] with a clove of garlick put in one of them and giving one every morning to the brown horse and Jenny Cammile. I have bled them and am now giving them physick as their legs swells after being taken up from grass. The rest of the horses are all much as usual. The cockey [11] is very well. Poor Ranger still has fits but not so often as he had them at first, neither are they so strong on him as at first. The rest of the dogs is all well.

We are all well here. I hope Your Honour and all with you are well. The new lad Henry Cross is returned from the Lock Hospital [12]. I have not heard from Your Honour since the letter I received on the 15th of September dated at Lauzanne 23rd August [13].

I am Your Honour's Servant at command

Will Bishop

Mr Row's father [14] was here a few days after I wrote my last letter, desired that I would enclose that small piece of paper to his son the first time [I] wrote to Your Honour.

On the 1st of this month the Duchess of Montrose [15] called at the Grove to enquire after Your Honour's health.

Abraham Shareman [16] the waterman is so ill in a decline that he will not get over it. The lads and Elizabeth Roberts agrees much better now than they did some time past.

Mrs Deale gives her duty to Your Honour & desires to be remembered to Richard. Hopes Your Honour is well & all with you are well. She is very well.

[On the address panel Morice has written] W. Bishop received 20th November, part answered and the whole 10th December 1783

Notes

1. Justice in the eighteenth century was, in a sense, a do-it-yourself affair. Bishop was an aggrieved person and so he got a warrant from a JP to detain his suspects and take them before a JP, possibly the same one who gave him the warrant, for which he might have had to pay. The trial could be an informal affair as seen here. If the accused admitted their guilt then they could be fined and told not to do it again. The same procedure was followed with the other theft described in this paragraph. The allocation of part of the fine to the poor of Chiswick was rather a nice idea.

2. Bear Key (rightly Quay) is near to London Bridge. It had been a corn market for many centuries but by this time was being replaced by the new Corn Market in Mark Lane.

3. The price that Bishop was paying for oats was a reasonable one but the price did not drop over the next few months as he optimistically told Morice it would. See *History of Agriculture and Prices in England* (ed J. Thorold Rogers, vol. 7, part 1, 1902, p. 188).

4. Straw paid for by the load not the truss in the following letter of 30 November.

5. The vestry consisted of the parishioners meeting to decide matters affecting the parish. The vestry was the only local governing body. By law parishes had to meet to set a poor rate which reflected their anticipated expenditure on poor relief, keeping of the work house, and 'out relief' for needy poor not in the workhouse. The rate was collected by the overseers of the poor who were appointed each year by the vestry meeting when they also appointed the two churchwardens. Since the rate was set under the Poor Law Acts of 1597 and 1601 (and revisions) it was subject to appeal to the Justices of the Peace at the Quarter Sessions as will be seen below.

6. There is no record in the vestry minutes for this period about a 'disturbance' caused by Mr Weatherstone nor notice of his burial in the Chiswick registers. His wife became the rate-payer in 1784.

7. The rapid return of the dry mouth is a sign of the return of the mercury poisoning, see Letter 2, note 3.

8. Tartar was probably too old to withstand the damage caused by the kick, see Letter 1, note 4.

9. 'Strangles' in horses is an acute bacterial infection. The cough would probably be associated with this and the swelling of the legs was a natural effect caused by bringing animals into a stable when they had been on grass. The effect of strangles was sometimes to cause broken-windedness in the horse afflicted, see Letter 8, note 7.

10. Commin cordial balls. Bishop may mean cumin balls here, cumin was used to combat swelling. Why Bishop added garlic is unclear.

11. Cocky. Probably a Cocker Spaniel, referred to in many letters under various similar pet names.

12. For Lock Hospital, see above, Letter 3, note 9.

13 This date for Morice being in Lausanne fits with the Letters 1 and 2, which are addressed to Lausanne.

14. From this it sounds as if Row junior was one of the Grove staff with Morice in Naples (see below, Letter 15, 29 November 1784).

15. The Duchess of Montrose was not a relation of Morice. She may have been enquiring as a near neighbour, as she and the Duke lived in nearby Twickenham. This is the first time she inquired after Morice's health, see also Letter 16, 4 February 1785, note 4.

16. Abraham Shareman (correctly Sherman) was apparently not a Grove man. His death is not in the Chiswick parish register.

Letter Five

The Grove 30th November 1783

Honoured Sir

On the 12th of November I received a letter from Rome, I carried it to Mr Saunders [1] immediately, and on the 17th I received that dated 21st October, on the 27th that dated 4th of November. About three weeks since Silver the coach horse fell lame on the off leg before, I give him three doses of physick, he is now quite sound. The little chestnut mare Rose in the park has been lame in both her fore feet & she is got well again. The bay mare geney cammile [Jenny Cammile] & the brown horse Little John their cough is much as it was. I am sadly afraid they are both touched in their wind as I have observed them to heave after water and they seldom or ever coughs but after water [2]. The blind cart horse is lame on the off leg before, the rest of the horses are all much as usual except old Emperor & he I thinks gets rather worse with his lameness, and the callous grows bigger & he goes more lamer on it than he did sometime back. The cock and all the dogs are all well, & glad to hear Your Honour is better and that all are well with Your Honour.

Coals being down at thirty three shillings the chaldron [3] I have got in ten chaldron from Mr Tremels [4] as I concluded that coals would get dearer as the winter advanced. I have entirely forgot if I ever sent Your Honour Mr Tremels Bill that was sent here last May, there was thirty chaldron of coals owing for then.

We have two calfs born since I wrote last to Your Honour

This year John Vaughan has received for walnuts & chestnuts clear of all expenses thirty seven pounds fifteen shillings [5], he means to pay the garden men with it as long as the money lasts. A few days after I wrote to Your Honour Abraham Sherman [6] died. Frances Gray of Pellmell [7] sent her bill in for garden seeds sent to the Grove last January charged three pound ten shillings.

Robert Carter wants a pair of leather breeches & boots.

John Weeden wants leather breeches & a stable hat.

Will Gould wants a stable hat, Henry Cross wants a hat.

And I should be glad to have a pair of breeches and a hat, and my great coat is almost wore out [8]. The last new lad that is by the week in Charles Slocumb's [9] place would be glad to know if he is to be hired by the year as it hinders him from getting any other place. I am Your Honour's Servant at Command
Will Bishop

Mrs Deale is glad to hear Richard & all is well with Your Honour. She has been ill with a cold this ten days past but is now getting better.

Mrs Chandler's bills are sent in. I have looked them over & they are all right, her year was up 22nd of this Month.

Thirty three load of hay at £3.15s.0d per load	£123.15s.0d
Forty five load of Wheat Straw at £1.13s.0d	£74.5s.0d
Nine load of Oat Straw at £1.7s.0d	£12.3s.0d
132 Bundles of tares at £0.1s.0d per bundle	£6.12s.0d
[Total]	£216.15s.0d
Mrs Chandler have received on Account	£125.0s.0d
The Balance due to her	£91.15s.0d

[Written on the address panel in Morice's hand] Received 1st January 1784 W. Bishop, answered 6th January

Notes

1. This is the first reference to Mr Saunders, who seems to have been a senior member of Morice's staff, although not resident at the Grove. He is mentioned frequently and Bishop seems to defer to him. He

was obviously a person of some authority, since here he received a letter from Morice, presumably containing instructions, and Bishop consults him about various matters, usually involving building matters. He was later 'determined' not to pay rates until the matter was properly settled, and also appealed at another time to the land tax commissioners. See letters nos 5–9, 14, 15.

2. Coughing after drinking cold water is a classic symptom of broken-windedness as Bishop observed. For broken-windedness see Letter 8, note 7.

3. A chauldron was a dry measure of volume, only used for coal by this time, when it consisted of 36 bushels.

4. Mr Tremells was apparently the usual coal merchant for the Grove; he is mentioned again in Letters 8 and 12.

5. Lysons in his *Environs of London* says that sometimes the fruit of the walnuts at the Grove produced £80 per annum (*Environs of London*, vol. 2, Middlesex, 1795, page 197). This year, and even more in 1784 when the yield was only £10.2s.6d (although clear of expenses), were obviously not as good.

6. Abraham Sherman the waterman is also mentioned in Letters 3 and 4, where his name is spelled Shermas and Shareman respectively.

7. Frances Gray of Pellmell. The firm of Samuel Gray and F. Gray of Pall Mall traded until about 1785. Samuel described himself in his will as a mustard seed and flower (flour?) seller. Perhaps Bishop bought mustard flour rather than the seed and used it for 'blistering' of the animals, see Letter 16, note 2. Thanks are due to Val Bott for the information on the Grays.

8. A man of Bishop's status would not usually have his clothes provided, his livery.

9. Slocumb had apparently left at some point before this. He seems to be a current member of staff in the fragment with Letter 2 of 25 August, although we do not know the actual date of the fragment. The new lad was John Hankins, see Letter 3, note 18.

10. Tares are cultivated vetch, used as fodder.

Letter Six

The Grove 4th January 1784 [original month deleted and illegible, new month written in by Morice]

Honoured Sir

On the 17th December I received Your Honour's letter with the drafts. I have spoke to Mr Saunders about the coach horse stable. Mr Saunders thinks it useless [1] as well as myself to take up any of the pavement to examine the ground as it is impossible there can be any water lodged there to cause the least dampness to any of the stalls in that stable, there being no well or drain or anything of that kind near it, the ground being entirely solid. There is a well under the saddle horse stable which belong to the pump in the passage.

It was a mistake of mine with regard to Mr Jullion's bill, his mentioning in his bill a repeater named perrigall [2] - a glass & repaired -7s, a repeater named Julion Leroy repaired & cleaned charged 18s 6d, I understood it to be two clocks repaired instead of watches, not knowing that he had repaired any of Your Honour's watches till I showed him the slip of paper Your Honour sent me. There is now two years' care of the clocks due to him the 25 of December last so that his bill now amounts to £5.9s.6d.

I have not seen any cart horses that are to be disposed of as yet but I should suppose that we could get two very good ones for about 18 or 20 pound a horse at Smithfield or any of the farmers or horse dealers who has those kind of horses to sell [3]. Spritely the blind cart horse is got quite sound again, the rest of the horses are all much as they was when I wrote to Your Honour last except the coach horse Smiler. He has got a slight cold & a running at his nose, he has no cough and eats & drinks as usual, so I hope it will soon go off. I give him James powders & Marshes & now & then a cordial ball [4]. Poor old Nickey is grown so weak & feeble that I think he cannot hold it out much longer. The cockey and all the dogs are all well.

We have now got five young heifers & calves & four cows so that we shall have nine cows & a bull. I should be glad to know if Your Honour means to rear any more cow calves or to dispose of them in future as well as the bull calves.

I had forgot to mention it to Your Honour till it was too late for me to have an answer from Your Honour about the garden men having their bread, beef &c at Christmas, but I have given it them as usual as I concluded that Your Honour meant that they should have it [5].

Mr Auckland has spoke to me for the money for the tithe of the hay [6] last year £3.12s.6d.

It is now two years since the drains in the meadows was cleaned out. They should be cleaned out again some time in February or March if your Honour approves of it, the cleaning the drains and cutting the rushes will cost about seven pounds.
[Against this paragraph concerning the drains is an X, see below]

I have hired John Hankins by the year as he has been kept in suspense so long and has behaved very well hither to. I have had the clothes that was Charles Slocumb's made fit for him, but the leather breeches & hats and boots must be new for him, & I have ordered Henry Cross to have the clothes that he was to have had when we had our clothes last.

Elizabeth Roberts have been very poorly with a cold and a rheumatic pain in one of her knees, she is now got better. Susan has got a kind of an ague fit every day, has had a cold but she is better than she was [7].
I am Your Honour's Servant at Command,
Will Bishop

[On the third, blank page, against the X above, in Morice's hand is written] Desired him to pay this & the next X out of the overplus of money remaining in his hands [there is no next X]

Mrs Deale is very well. Desires to be remembered to Richard

[Written on the address panel in Morice's hand; perhaps writing in these dates prompted him to correct Bishop's date] W. Bishop received 6th February 1784, answered 17th February. H

Notes

1. Bishop spelled this word 'youslesse'.
2. The Perigals were watchmakers of London, Jullion was a watch and clockmaker of Brentford. Julien Leroy and his son were French clockmakers.
3. Purchase of horses: this sounds as if Morice had written to say that Bishop could buy them after he had told Morice he needed to (Letter 3).
4. Smiler probably had mild equine influenza. James's powder was probably largely powdered antimony oxide, perhaps mixed with calcium phosphate. It was used to reduce fever, as (probably) was Marshes powder. This was a mixture of iron oxide (rust) and cassia, amongst other things. For cordial balls, see above, Letter 4 of 30 October, note 10. It seems that Bishop believed that if one medicine was good, three might be better.
5. It sounds from this as if Bishop was partly responsible for the 'garden men', see pages 11 to 12, and 17 above, and he was accounting for their wages in Letter 15 in 1784 although Vaughan was going to pay their wages from the money for walnuts in 1783.
6. Mr Auckland was the receiver for the Duke of Devonshire in Chiswick. The tithes he was calling for were due to the Duke of Devonshire as lay rector of the parish. Tithes were originally an annual payment of a proportion of the annual produce of the parish to support the church and was payable by all parishioners. By the eighteenth century the payment had often been commuted to cash as it had been here and the rectors of many parishes were laymen and had no religious connection with the church. Mr Auckland is mentioned several times in the letters.
7. Ague is often used to describe malaria, but whatever Susan had it was almost certainly not this, which is not really prevalent in London.

Letter Seven

The Grove 26th January 1784

Honoured Sir

On the 9th of January I received your letter dated the 10th December with
the draft for the poor rates [1] - the poor rates are not as yet settled, Mr
Saunders is determined not to pay anything until it is settled before a
bench of Justices, which we expect will be in the course of ten days or
a fortnight. I have sent the James Powders [2] to Mr Kerby's on the 12th
instant. The places over the stables intended for oats are still at the same
liberty as ever they was. There is but one of them that has ever been made
use of as a dressing room, & that only at a time when it was not wanted.
Oats have been at a great price since October 1782 [3]. If they had been
any ways reasonable I should have ordered in a large quantity long before
this, but I have been in expectation of their being cheaper as no one could
think that they would have kept up so long as they have after so fine a
harvest as we had last year.

I have consulted Mr Salter about giving Junice the mercury [4] in small
quantities. He advises me to wait until the Spring when the weather is
more mild, as we have very sharp frost here & has been for this month

past. The people have all gone on very regular for some time past. Whoever acquainted Your Honour that I am always out both forenoon & afternoon when it is not stable time, lays under a great mistake. If they had told you that I had lain at home now and then at nights they would have told much nearer the truth than they have by telling you that I am out forenoons & afternoons. What confusion Mary can have created in our family a second time [5] I cannot conceive as she has never been at the Grove since she left it in the year 1780. Neither do I intend she ever shall while I live.

On the 23rd I received Your Honour's letter with the draft for £33.

Mrs Phillips is very poorly, all the dogs that was Mrs Morice's [6] are all alive & well. Mrs Phillips told me that she had wrote to Your Honour about a week since, desired me to tell you that Cathern Reynolds was dead, she died the 27th December last & Mrs Wingood died the 16th of this month [7]. Mrs Phillips told me that Robert Bye was married & has a child, he was married a twelvemonth before Mrs Phillips knew anything of it, that he is still with his master [8].

A few days after I wrote my last letter to Your Honour poor old Nickey went off, he was quite un[illegible]able two or three days before he died. I conclude that he was near thirty years old by the account old Paul told me when I was at Werrington [9].

Smiler is got quite well of the cold and the running at the nose. Old Sultan the coach horse has strained the back sinews of his off leg behind, he is something better than he was. I have applied the Steers Opodeldoc [10] to it. The other horses are all much as usual. Gillman has had a touch of the canker[11] in one of his feet but I have stopped it. Twister has again had his old complaint, is now got better. I treated him as before with Clysters Bathing [12] &c,

Ranger has still fits though not so often as he had some time back. I have given him some drops of Assafateda [13] which Mr Norbon the Dog Doctor advised me to do, the rest of the dogs are all well & the Cockey.

Betty Roberts is so lame with the rheumatism that she cannot walk without a stick [14]. Susan has done the work for her since she has been so lame. Betty Roberts complained of the room being very cold where she lay, the room that John Boham used to lay in. I spoke to Jane to let her have some other room that was more warmer and for her not to have so far to walk up and down stairs as she was so lame. Jane has put her in to Mr Allan's room to lay [15].

I am Your Honour's Servant at Command

Will Bishop

Mrs Deale gives her Duty to Your Honour, is glad Your Honour is better. She is sorry to hear that Richard has been ill but is glad that he is better. She is very well, hopes Your Honour and all with you are well.

Bills brought in

Joseph Horn's Bill			£15.6s.0d

[written after 'Bill' by Morice] a draft 4 Mar 1784

Nicholas Taylor cooper's Bill [16]		X	£4.4s.6d
Edward Gould Bill		X	£4.17s.0d

[written below this line by Morice] draft to Mr Bull [17]

William Salter's Bill two years standing			£19.2s.0d

[written below this line by Morice, with WB after the figure] a draft 4 Mar

William Curtis's Bill standing from April 1782			£19.9s.11d
John Bodenham for two hats a Bill [18]		X	£1.9s.0d
Charles Blake the Tin Man's Bill [19]		X	£4.0s.6d
Robert Richin's Bill [20]			£34.4s.6d

[written below this line by Morice with WB after the sum] a draft to Mr Bull

Henry James has given me a Bill, the glazier at Chiswick standing from January 1782 to July 1782. I knows of nothing that he has done at the Grove since your Honour paid him at the Grove his Bill is charged £2.16s.3d

[Below this is written by Morice] Those X by a draft to W Bishop 4th Mar 1784 amount to £14.11s.0d

[On the address panel Morice has written] W. Bishop received 22nd February, answered 4th March [and deleted] Mr Malliam received 22nd February

Notes

1. Apparently someone had appealed against the rate set (see above, Letter 4, note 5). It was still not settled by Letter 9, 25 March.
2. Since James's powders were used for people as well as animals this was perhaps why Bishop was asked to send some to Mr Kerby, see Letter 6, note 4.
3. The price of oats certainly had not dropped as Bishop had prophesied. See Letter 4, note 3.

4. As seen above mercury, in the form of mercurous chloride, had been used before on poor Junice; this presumably is what Bishop means. Metallic mercury has no medicinal use. Mr Salter was frequently consulted on veterinary matters.

5. We do not know who Mary is. Perhaps a previous member of staff with whom Bishop was at issue. It sounds as if Bishop knew perfectly well who had been telling tales about him. The matter obviously concerned him, perhaps he feared that Morice would take it seriously and dismiss him. It is interesting to see that Bishop refers again here to the household as 'the family' as he also does in Letter 1. If 'Mary' was a previous member of staff it seems that not all of them would have been happy, or welcome to come back (see below Letter 13, note 7). It probably depended on the circumstances under which they left.

6. By Mrs Morice Bishop means Anne Morice, Morice's half-sister who died in 1777. Mrs Phillips was Elizabeth Phillips and had been a servant of Anne Morice, perhaps her lady's maid since she was left Anne Morice's clothing and £80 a year, as well as a gold bracelet, some linen, furniture and other wearing apparel. She was known to Morice, who had a good opinion of her and her honesty. In a letter to Sir William Lee in 1780 he describes how his sister had years before lost a bank note for £20 and thought she had accidentally thrown it in the fire. Mrs Phillips had just found it in a work basket of Anne Morice and obviously given it to Morice. She had also at some point given to Lee a £2,000 bank stock bond which no one knew she had. Morice suggests to Lee that her honesty deserves a reward and that she be given some old linen which had belonged to his sister, which he admits is of little value but which it will please her to have. (Will proved 27 Nov. 1777, PROB 11/1036; Centre for Buckinghamshire Studies, D/LE/D/8/24). Mrs Phillips evidently knew Morice's staff and must have been living fairly close to the Grove since Bishop went to see her, see Letters 16 and 17. She was apparently also looking after Anne Morice's dogs. Perhaps Anne Morice was as fond of animals as her brother.

7. Catherine Reynolds had been a servant of Anne Morice and is mentioned in her will, where she was left an annuity of £10 for life as well as some furniture and linen [PROB 11/1036, pr. 27 November 1777]. Mrs Wingood was left an annuity in Morice's will; she may perhaps have been a past member of his or Anne Morice's staff.

8. Robert Bye was a lad of four or five years of age in 1766 and was then in the household of Anne Morice (half-sister of Morice). He was the son of Mary and John Bye, who were perhaps servants of Anne Morice. Robert was left several annuities (a total of £55) in Anne Morice's will, these to be paid to Elizabeth

Phillips on his behalf until he was twenty-one years of age, to be used for his maintenance and education, or if Elizabeth died, to be paid to his mother. At a proper age he was to be apprenticed to a trade or business, and by a codicil he was left £500 to be paid when he was twenty-four years of age to set him up in a trade. He was duly apprenticed as seen in this letter because he was still with his master and indeed married. He did receive the £500 since his receipt for the money still survives, dated 1786 when he was presumably aged twenty-four. (Will proved 27 Nov. 1777, PROB 11/1036; Centre for Buckinghamshire Studies, D/LE/D/1/57). This concern for a young dependant was paralleled by a similar provision in Morice's will, where he left John Allan junior, an apprentice to Messrs Lane and Bicknell of Cheapside, linen drapers, and perhaps the son of his senior servant John Allan, £500 when his apprenticeship should be expired.

9. For Will Bishop at Werrington, see above, page 10 The horse, Nickey, had reached what is about the maximum age for a horse.

10. Steers Opodeldoc was a camphorated soap liniment which included ammonia. A similar liniment is still used for sprains and strains.

11. Canker is a very serious condition in a horse, although Bishop seems to make light of it here. It is a disease of the foot, usually caused by poor conditions underfoot and bad management, although one would be sorry to think that was the cause here. The treatment is to cut out the infected area and disinfect it.

12. A clyster is an enema.

13. Assafateda, properly asafoetida, was used in humans to relieve flatulence and as a general sedative and for hysteria. It was not usually used for animals, where other similarly acting substances were used.

14. Betty Roberts was reported as lame with rheumatism in the previous letter and is reported as suffering from various degrees of lameness in subsequent letters. It seems unlikely that her final illness (see Letter 17) had anything to do with this 'rheumatism'.

15. Jane Power, see page 14.

16. What this work was for is explained in Letter 10, of 29 April, note 4.

17. For Richard Bull paying bills, see above in the Introduction to the letters, page 9.

18. John Bodenham is first mentioned here and twice afterwards, in Letters 8 and 12. Each reference is in connection with hats for the stable staff; he was obviously used regularly by Morice for this purpose.

19. The 'Tin Man' was probably a tinsmith, a maker of goods in tin plate.

20. Morice queried this bill with Bishop, see Letter 10. Richins was one of the vets used by Bishop, the other was Mr Salter.

Letter Eight

The Grove 23rd February 1784

Honoured Sir

On the 2nd of this month I received your letter dated 6th of January with the draft for Mary Chandler [1]. On the same day we had a sad misfortune happen to one of Philis's young pups that was born since you left England. Thomas Hickman [2] was in the park drawing dung & all his dogs with him as they commonly are when the horses are at work, some of the coach hors [sic: house?] dogs being in the park at the same time they ran after the puppy, frighted it so that the pup ran under the cart wheel and was killed on the spot.

On Saturday night the 7th it being spring tides and there being a large quantity of ice in the Thames which came with such violence that it carried away the greatest part of Barker rails [3] next the Thames by the summerhouse. It came with such force as to break three of the posts level with the ground, carried them & the rails together with all the iron work belonging to them down the Thames. The next day I got five fishermen with their boats and got up all the iron work that was carried away & all the principal part of the old timber, which would have been carried away & lost the next tide if it had not been taken up on the Sunday morning after.

We have had the hardest winter here I ever remember, continually sharp frost & a great deal of snow for nine weeks [4]. Last Saturday the frost broke & we now have a fine thaw. Would Your Honour like that Mrs Morgan should repair the railing that is carried away by the ice or Mr Saunders [5] to repair it. The timber must be all new as far as the ice has damaged it, but all the iron work will do again

The weather being so very hard that there was not much to be done in the garden I thought it a good opportunity for drawing out all our dung while the ground was hard as the wheels would not cut up the park as in milder weather. For this reason I hired a cart horse for a month at 12 shillings per week to help our cart horses draw the dung out &c.

My reason for not ordering in twenty chaldron of coals at the time I had in the last ten chaldron was because we had a few chaldron in the house & ten chaldron more was as many as the coal hole in the house would possibly hold, & as Your Honour did not like that any coals should be laid in any place out of the house when you was at the Grove I thought it would have been very imprudent for me to have had any coals laid anywhere out of the house at a time when you was not at the Grove.

Oats has kept up at a great price ever since October 1782 when they then was at 19s 6d per quarter [6] which is a long price for oats, and no one at that time could have thought that it was possible for oats to have kept up to the price as they have done so long. And another thing was the harvest in 1782 was so bad that the oats was so indifferent at that time in general that they would not have kept all the year, as soon as they are any ways reasonable I will order in a hundred quarter at once.

The coach horse Silver is quite sound. He is not a-going to have the same kind of lameness as Junice and the rest of them. It was nothing but humours which the physick carried off. As to those horses going broken winded I cannot account for as those complaints often comes on without any visible sign or mismanagement, & most horses that are got by a broken winded horse or out of a broken winded mare in general goes off broken winded sooner or later. And there is but few of those colts but what is subjected to this complaint some time of their life if they lives to be 10 or twelve years old [7].

As to hiring a staid man to look after the stable people in my absence [8], I really think it useless as I am so seldom from home & I don't think it possible there can be any pranks played with the horses in the stable without my finding it out, & I never trust them out on the road with the horses to exercise by themselves for fear they should play any pranks when I was not with them, but if Your Honour wishes to hire any steady man I have not the least objection to it.

Jane gives her duty to Your Honour, she takes care of all the bedding, blankets &c that no moths gets in them & likewise those things in the clothes press [9].

The coach horse Sultan is better with regard to the strain he got. The rest of the horses are all much as they was, and all the dogs are much as usual, the cockey is very well.

Elizabeth Roberts is got better, has now just begun to do her work in the kitchen again.

Mr Townly [10] desired his compliments to Your Honour

I am Your Honour's Servant at Command

Will Bishop

Roger Tremells Bill for Coals

1782	June 15th	10½ Chaldron at 4s.2d	£21.0s.d
		Metage & Lighterage	£1.2s.0d
		Porterage & Carriage	£2.7s.0d
	December 20th	10½ Chaldron at 4s 2d	£21.0s.0d
		Metage & Lighterage	£1.2s.0d
		Porters & Carriage	£2.7s.0d
1783	May 3rd	10½ Chaldron at 3s 4d	£17.0s.0d
		Metage & Lighterage	£1.2s.d
		Porters & Carriage	£2.7s.0d
	November 21st	10½ Chaldron at 3s 3d	£16.10s.0d
		Metage & Lighterage	£1.2s.0d
		Porters & Carriage	£2.5s.8d
		[Total]	£89.4s.8d

[In Morice's hand] Sent Mr Tremells a draft 11 May 1784 [11]

John Bodenham's Bill for four Stable hats [12]	£3.0s.0d
William Balls Bill for 5 pair of Breeches [13]	£6.5s.0d
[Total]	£9.5s.0d

[Below Morice has written] Sent 3rd May 1784 to pay this with draft of £25 - a surplus £15. 15s. 0d. advised W. Bishop

Mrs Deale gives her Duty to Your Honour. She has been but poorly for the last fortnight past, has had a cold with a pain in her head. She desires to be remembered to Richard, she is now got better.

[Written on the address panel by Morice] W. Bishop with Mr Tremells bill, answered 11th May 1784. H

Notes

1. Mrs Chandler was a corn factor, see Letter 4.

2. The work that Thomas Hickman was doing, drawing dung, was what Bishop said would be difficult that year because he really needed extra carthorses

(Letter 3, 20 September 1783). This was presumably a hint to Morice to authorise buying two more. If so it didn't work because Bishop was saying in Letter 6 in the following 4th January what the cost of two horses would be. This letter seems to show that he had decided (perhaps on his own authority) to hire a cart plus horses together with a carter. Hickman continued to do work at the Grove into the summer, see Letter 11, 24 June 1784. Perhaps he was being hired by the week as John Weedon had been for a time. He is also referred to in the following letter.

3. Barker's Rails. From documents in the Duke of Devonshire's records at Chatsworth these were along the Thames just past the Grove estate, on the other side of Burlington Lane where it came down to the Thames and by the summer house referred to. (Peter Hammond,' Barkers Rails and the University Boat Race', *Brentford and Chiswick Local History Journal*, 14, 2005, pp. 26–7). From what is said here the implication is that the railings along the Thames fringing the Grove estate may also have been known loosely as Barkers Rails, at least at this time. They were, later, in 1856, the point at which the Oxford and Cambridge boat race started so that by then the 'Rails' must have been an easily distinguished place.

4. The winter of 1783/4 was exceptionally cold over most of England, beginning in late December with no proper thaw until late February. The hard frost would explain the earlier reference to the ice floes.

5. This probably means shall Mr Saunders arrange for it to be seen to. As a senior man he would not have carried out the repair himself, see Letter 5, note 1.

6. The price of oats was a recurring topic; it seems as though Bishop knew that Morice was concerned about it, see Letter 7, note 3.

7. Broken-windedness in horses is sometimes the effect of having suffered strangles. It is shown by a difficulty or noisiness in breathing, with a curious double expiration of air. See Letter 4, note 9.

8. 'Hiring a … man' in Bishop's absence sounds as though it was Morice's response to the stories of Bishop's absences (see Letter 7, note 5). Bishop sounds rather offended by the idea despite his protestations of agreement.

9. For Jane, see above, page 14.

10. Mr John Towneley was a neighbour of Morice. He owned Corney House just down the river from the Grove.

11. This draft is referred to in a note at the end of the next letter. It appears that at least sometimes Morice saved up Bishop's letters to answer at intervals, or perhaps ill health caused him to delay answering them.

12. Bodenham is also mentioned in Letters 7 and 12. See Letter 7 for comment.

13. William Ball is mentioned once more (Letter 12). He was apparently another supplier of livery clothes.

Letter Nine

The Grove 25th March 1784

Honoured Sir

On the 17th instant I received Your Honours letter dated the 17th of February.
I am happy to hear that Your Honour is got so much better & that all with
you is so well. John Wood has been ill of the flux. He is now got quite well [1].
The new man John Hankins has had a pain in his side for some time & now
it is fell in to his groin & swollen very much. Mr Curtis thinks it will break.
Susan has been troubled with a pain in her head the greatest part of the
winter. Elizabeth Roberts is very well with regard to her health but is still a
little lame in one knee with a rheumatic pain. The rest of us are all well [2].

I am very sorry to acquaint Your Honour that I have at last lost my poor
old dog Ranger. He died last Sunday night in one of the fits that he was
troubled with. Jully the little bitch is very lame on one of her hind legs by
some hurt she got while she was up at heat with some of the other bitches.
The cockey & all the rest of the dogs is well. The coach horse Sultan is got
the better of the strain, & the rest of the horses are all much as usual. We
have lost the old cat that used to be in the saddle horse stable. He went away
about three weeks back & has not been heard of since.

Two of the stones belonging to the stone steps at the door nex[t] the
library are broke & shivered to pieces by the late hard frost we had.

The cart horses are certainly wanted as much in the summer as in the
winter, but at the same time we may be able to do without buying by now,

and then hiring when they are wanted, & I should much rather that you should see them before they was bought [3].

After I have paid for draining the meadows, & Mr Auckland [4] & Mr Jullion I shall not have above ten pound in cash left & a draft for £33 besides the draft for £35 to pay the poor rates which is not as yet paid [5]. Mr Saunders was at the Bench of Justice last Saturday. It was not settled, the Justice put it off until the next Bench Day when it will be settled what must be paid.

The butter account amounts to no more than £12.13s.8¾ d [6]. We have not been able to make any butter since December last having only two cows that give milk & two calves to suck them [7]. It is impossible to make much butter while the calves is rearing. Now the calves are to be disposed of there will be of course more butter made. We have just now another cow calved, a bull calf.

Last year myself being under the necessity of having on account twenty five pound and the same this year [8] and the money I have advanced to the stable people on account has reduced all the overplus of the money & drafts I have received.

Has received this year on account [9]

To	Robert Carter	£10.10s.0d
	William Gould	£4.4s.0d
	John Weeden	£3.3s.0d
	Henry Chroust	£3.3s.0d

It is very odd that Henry called himself Cross and he says that he spells his name Chroust.

Robert Carter gives his duty to Your Honour. He should be glad if Your Honour would give him leave to go home into Suffolk for a fortnight to see his friends when the horses are at grass
I am Your Honour's Servant at Command
Will Bishop
Mrs Deale gives her duty to your Honour. She [is] extremely happy that Your Honour is got s[o much] better than you was, & to hear that Richard [and all] with you is so well. She has been but poor[ly and] had a pain in her face & a cold but is now [better]. In hope to see Your Honour & all with you safe [back in] England again soon.

[Written on the address panel by Morice] W. Bishop, answered 11th May 1784 with account butter sold. H

Notes

1. It sounds as if John Wood was a member of staff but he is not mentioned again so his status remains a mystery. He probably had ordinary diarrhoea, perhaps from food poisoning.

2. With three staff far from well, Bishop's statement that the rest of the staff were well sounds like optimism. Hankins did not get better; reports of his illness are given in many subsequent letters, with him getting worse in nearly every one. In the last letter in which he is referred to, that of 4 April 1785 (Letter 17) every day is expected to be his last. Since he was taken on at the end of November 1783 Bishop only got three months' steady work from him. From the descriptions of the progress of his illness he could have been suffering from a tubercular infection of the spine, perhaps from drinking unpasteurised milk; see Letters 10, 12, 13, 14, 15 and 16. Mr Curtis was the doctor always consulted by Bishop (see above, Letter 3, note 8). See the previous letter for reference to the freezing weather.

3. This note about the horses seems to be answering a question by Morice and is part of the ongoing dialogue about carthorses started in Letter 3, 20 September 1783.

4. For Mr Auckland see above, Letter 6.

5. The amount payable for the previous year's poor rate was apparently not settled, see Letter 7, note 1. It seems unlikely that anyone minded not paying. Mr Saunders had gone to hear the appeal. See Letter 14.

6. Butter sold at about 6*d* per pound at this time so this would represent about 500 lbs of butter, quite a lot. We do not know how long it took to accumulate this sum, of course. If they were making butter then they must have had a dairy maid of course, or at least someone acting as such (see above, p. 14).

7. The implication here seems to be that they kept very few cows, perhaps just enough to (normally) keep them in butter and milk.

8. This seems to be saying that Will Bishop was paying himself from the unallocated funds at his disposal, and that he was getting at least £25 per year. This sum would indicate a status more like a bailiff than a groom, (see J. Jean Hecht, *The Domestic Servant in Eighteenth Century England*, 1956, pp. 142, 145) although wages varied so much that status is difficult to estimate from any particular wage.

9. See Letter 18, note 1: it looks as if the stable staff received a wage of £10 10*s* per year.

Letter Ten

The Grove 29th [deletion] 1784 [followed in Morice's hand by] should be
April [1]

Honoured Sir

I received Your Honour's letter dated March the 4th. Richins' [2] bill was
for a whole year, the bill before this last was only nine months, which
makes the difference between the last bill & the bill before it [3]. John
Vaughan having had six new tubs for the orange trees, that cost four
pounds two shillings, or the cooper's bill would have been only two
shillings and sixpence for repairing two pails [4]. The winter have been
so very sharp & the snow laying on the ground so long that the pigeons
have had more barley given them than if the winter had been more mild
[5]. There has not been a fowl more kept than those that Your Honour
left to be taken care of. Mr James [6] bill arises from the 15th of January
1782 to July the 17th 1782, I conclude that this bill was due to him at the
same time he give Your Honour his last bill. It is so long back that I cannot
recollect only two of the articles that is in his bill which I know he did, but
I thought that when Your Honour paid him his last bill, there was nothing
more due to him. As I don't recollect that he has done anything since Your
Honour paid him, this bill must be due to him at the same time he was
paid the last bill.

Oronooko has had a complaint fell in to his back and loins attended
with such a weakness that he could not get up when he was down
without help. I bled him & give him three doses of physick & I have put

a strengthening plaster over his loins. He is now much better than he was and is able to get up without help [7]. The gray horse Gilman has just thrown out a sandcrack [8] on the near foot. The rest of the horses are all much as usual. Jully is still very lame, and one of the young puppies is lame by one of the cart horses treading on her in the night time. The rest of the dogs is all well & the Cockey is very well [9].

It is very extraordinary that the white bitch Philliss was brought to bed with one puppy only & no one ever knew that she was with pup, or that she had ever been lined until she was brought to bed.

The new man John Hankins is still very ill. The swelling in his groin is not broke. He some time back was very desirous to go to St George's Hospital. I sent him. The surgeons told him that nothing could be done for him until it was broke. The enclosed slip of paper is Mr Curtis's opinion of his case [10].

Timothy Newman [11] the Collector of the Land Tax has been here for the Land Tax due Lady Day last		£55.8s.0d
Mr Wopshott [12] for Window tax	X	£12.3s.0d
House tax	X	£7.10s.0d
Mr Sich [13] for Church rates	X	£5.16s.6d
Thomas Dancer [14] for the byways for the ensuing year		£12.6s.3d
John Frances for three quarterly Bills sent in	X	£4.4s.10d

[written below this line in Morice's hand] Paid these four X a draft to WB 1st June [15] 1784 £29.14s.4d

I asked Mr Newman the reason why the land tax was rose from thirty five to fifty five pounds eight shillings. He says it is on account of the poor rate being rose, as they always rate them so much in the pound according to what they are rated in the poor book, & the same with regard to the Byways. The money paid last year for the byways was no more than six pounds eighteen shillings & threepence. I told both Mr Newman and Mr Dancer that it could not be paid until such time as the poor rates was finally settled, which I suppose will be the next Bench Day. There is another half years poor rates due at Lady Day last.

Last Thursday there came three men here to enquire after Robert Carter [16]. Robert luckily happened not to be in the way when they came, they being so very desirous to see Robert but would by no means tell me who they was nor where they came from nor what they wanted with him. I had some supposition [suspicion?] that there was something

more than I knew of. I knew that Robert was gone to Brentford & I sent
one of the other lads to meet him to tell him that there was three men
came after him and ordered him to keep out of the way till I could find
out what they wanted with him

When they found that they could by no means get to see him they told
me that they came from Greenwich & was parish officers, that they came
to take Robert up for a bastard child sworn to him by an Elizabeth Tanner.
The child is about fifteen months old, and she is big with another which
the Officers says is his likeways as the girl tells them. This is the woman
that was reported to be married to Robert when you was abroad last. The
Officers told me that they will take ten pounds for the child that is born and
for Robert to take his chance for the second, whether she will swear to him
or not, or they will take twenty-two pounds and give him a free discharge
of both the children from any further trouble or expense. As Robert was so
lucky as not to be taken that day, he means to keep within the gates until he
hears from Your Honour. I found by the Officers that they are determined
to take him in case it is not settled by some means so I expect every day to
have another visit by some of the Greenwich gentlemen. The following is a
copy of a few lines that Robert desired me to send to Your Honour.

*Honoured Sir I beg pardon for what have so lately abruptly occurred to me. In
case Your Honour does not mean to order my discharge, I don't wish to leave
my place and as I have not a friend in the world nor any money to advance, I
request Your Honour will be so amicable as to put it in William Bishop's power
to adjust the affair for me, and as I have on a former occasion experienced
Your Honour's benevolence I don't wish to impose, therefore I hope Your
Honour will accept this as a pledge of my sincerity & fidelity in repaying you
when my ability will admit. So, Honoured Sir, I hope you will take this into
consideration as your petitioner will take care and not be guilty of the like
again and as in duty bound shall ever pray* [16].

Mrs Deale is very well, desires to be remembered to Richard. She hopes that
Your Honour and all with Your Honour is well
I am Your Honour's Servant at Command
Will Bishop

We have had a very cold backward spring here with a great deal of rain. The
trees & the hedges are but just now coming out in leaf [17].

[Written on the address panel by Morice] W. Bishop 2nd April 1784,
answered 4th June [18]

Notes

1. Will Bishop seems to have had problems with dates sometimes, see also Letters 1, 4, 6 and 11 as well as this one. Perhaps there is slight exasperation in the terse 'should be April' in this letter and the note on Letter 12 (see below). On the other hand Morice seems to have had problems too, see note 6 below.

2. Richins was one of the vets consulted by Bishop, the other was Mr Salter, both of Richmond.

3. Another example of Morice asking about a bill. He obviously kept a close eye on expenditure.

4. The cooper's bill referred to is probably that of Letter 3, see also Letter 7, note 16.

5. These were presumably domesticated pigeons unless Morice fed wild wood pigeons. Morice obviously felt that they were spending more on corn for 'fowl' than they should be.

6. Mr James was probably the glazier, see Letter 7.

7. This use of a plaster to strengthen a weak back or loins is not unusual. The name Oronooko should probably be more correctly Orinoco.

8. A sandcrack is a crack in the horn of the hoof, extending down from the top of the hoof where the horn is formed, equivalent to the nail bed in a human nail. Treatment is long and complicated.

9. From the way the 'cockey', presumably a cocker spaniel, is referred to the impression is given that it was an irrepressible dog, perhaps a particular favourite of Morice's.

10. Mr Curtis was the local doctor consulted by Bishop when necessary (see above, previous letter).

11. The collectors were appointed by the land tax commissioners and were not parish officers. Timothy Newman did live in the parish and attended vestry meetings. The land tax was based on the value of the land occupied, based on a valuation made originally in 1692.

12. The window and house taxes were national taxes collected by local appointees. Both were first levied in 1696. The window tax was based on the number of windows in a house but the exact rules varied over time. The house tax was a flat-rate tax which was payable by occupiers of all inhabited houses which were assessed for church and poor rates. The two taxes were assessed together on the same form for the first time in 1784, which may account for the fact that they were being collected together. Mr Wapshott was one of the churchwardens in 1783, he was also the local butcher.

13. The church rate had been set at 3*d* in the pound as it had been the previous year. Mr Sich was one of the churchwardens in 1784.

14. Mr Dancer was presumably Surveyor of the Highways for the parish since he was collecting the highway rate. The surveyor (or surveyors) were appointed by the vestry but no appointment was recorded in the vestry minutes at this time. Dancer regularly attended vestry meetings. He was a market gardener, see also illustration 19.

15. This date should be 1 July, see letter of 29 November when Bishop acknowledges getting the draft.

16. Robert Carter does not seem to have denied that he was responsible for Elizabeth Tanner's first child, which presumably occurred when they were 'married'. As the father he would be responsible under the Settlement Act of 1662 for paying for the upkeep of the child. A bastard born in a parish acquired the right of settlement which meant that the parish was legally bound to provide poor relief, i.e. upkeep in this case. The Greenwich parish officers were anxious to find someone other than the parish to pay for the child's upkeep. Asking for a lump sum was usually the way to cover this. Bishop's protective attitude, hiding Carter from the Greenwich officers, is rather charming. See also Letters 12, 16 and 20.

17. The spring of 1784 was generally very cold. After the thaw in February the cold weather returned in early March and lasted through most of the month until early April, after which the rains mentioned by Bishop set in. See *Records of the Seasons, etc.* collected by T. H. Baker (1883).

18. This date must be wrong if the letter was written at the end of April. The hand is very shaky, perhaps Morice was ill. Since Bishop wrote roughly once per month this letter should be about the end of April. There seems (now) to be no May letter.

Letter Eleven

The Grove 24th [month deleted] 1784 [Morice has written below] should be June

Honoured Sir

I received Your Honour's letter dated the 25th May with the two drafts. On Friday last Thomas Hickman the carter [1] lost one of the young puppies that was born since you left England, brother to that which was killed by the cart last winter. Thomas went to Turnham Green to take home some horses which I borrowed to help draw the hay in. The puppy followed him as far as the Packhorse [2] when some strange dog ran after him and frighted the puppy. He took off towards Hammersmith and has not been heard of since. I have had him advertised in the papers & cried by the crier, a guinea reward.

On Tuesday poor old Hasty met with a dreadful misfortune, she broke her thigh just below the stiffle [3]. How it happened God knows. I put her down in to the meadow with the rest of the park horses in the morning. She then was very well. In the evening I went to let them up as usual. I found her standing by herself not far from the shade with her thigh broke and shattered to pieces. I went for Richins to see if there was no possibility of saving her.

Richins told me that it was impossible for any man to save her. I give her some opium and had her put out of her misery by the same method as poor old Diamond was when he had the same misfortune in the park some years back. I am so unhappy and vexed about the dog and poor Hasty that I can scarce think of anything else at present. I pray God that

Your Honour was once more arrived safe in England again, for I think there is nothing but misfortunes happens to me latterly.
I am Your Honour's Servant at Command
Will Bishop

Mr Bull & his daughter [4] came here today. I conclude Mr Bull will acquaint Your Honour the particular what has happened to Joseph Vickers [5] on Wednesday morning about half after two o'clock.

[Written on the address panel by Morice] W. Bishop Received 16th July [6] answered 25th [blank] 1784

Notes

1. Thomas Hickman seems to be a semi permanent member of staff at this point, see Letter 8, note 2.
2. The Packhorse Inn is probably the inn on the corner of the High Road and Acton Lane now known as the Old Packhorse, not the Packhorse and Talbot.
3. The stiffle or correctly the stifle is the equine equivalent of the knee joint. Bishop does not say how he put Hasty down, it is as though he did not want to spell it out to Morice.
4. For Mr Bull and his daughter see Appendix 1. Bishop apparently wrote to the Bulls at times, see next letter.
5. The incident with Joseph Vickers is described in Letter 13 of 20 August.
6. This letter thus took one month to get to Naples. The answer of 25 July is acknowledged by Bishop in his letter of 20 August.

Letter Twelve

[Top of sheet removed. Dated in modern hand 26 April 1784, this is correctly 26 July, see below, cover note by Morice]

Immediately wrote to tell Mr Bull that the Dog was found [1] that he may acquaint you of it as Mr Bull told me that he should write to Your Honour in a day or two, otherwise I should have wrote sooner to have told you that the Dog was found, & that John Weeden had got the small pox broke out on him [2]. He has had them so favourable that he walked about all the time & is now perfect well. I got William Pitt [3] to come by the week while Weeden was ill of the small pox.

John Hankins is seemingly no worse than he was a month back [4]. The head surgeon of St Georges Hospital told him that his case was such that if he was to be confined in the Hospital it would shorten his days. He lays in the room where John Brown used to lay [5].

Elizabeth Roberts is much as usual but still lame & not able to do anything.

I tried the Steers Opodildoc [6] at first to July's leg, there is a callous formed on the joint which makes her go a little stiff on it, but she is very little lame with it. After I tried the Opodildoc I put a strengthening plaster all round the joint which helped her greatly. When the little bitch Flippant was put up at her heat some time back she broke out through the window and stole Dog and unluckily she proves with pup. The Cockey and all the rest of the dogs is well. The horses are all much as usual.

John Vaughan says that the cypress trees are kept together & the poles replaced to the cedars as they dropped. As to the padlock being kept on the gate by the summer house door there never has been one since you left England, nor for some time before [7].
[line(s) lost at top]
shut. The latter end of last month, coals being down at thirty two shillings per chaldron I ordered in twenty chaldron for which Mr Trimells has sent his bill for them, charged £38.15s. 4d

Draft for money has been sent for all the bills except
William Balls [8] for five pair of leather breeches charged   £6.5s.0d
John Bodenham [9] for four stable hats charged   £3.0s.0d
Henry James Bill at Chiswick charged   £2.16s.3d

If I am not mistaken I sent the account of them in a letter dated the 23rd of February last [10].
I have a little bill of Mr Sardgerso [torn] and Smith at Kensington for trifles done for Mrs Morice [11] £0.16s.6d.

All the other bills that has come to my hand are all paid except those two bills which I sent the account of the 10th of June last [12]. The enclosed bills Mr Allan left when he was in England last. I know nothing of them. The remainder of the bills which Allan left I enclosed to Your Honour some time last summer.

I have only one draft left for board wages besides that which was returned to me last April. I shall want about fourteen pounds to pay for the second crop of hay the beginning of September next. John Vaughan not being able to keep all the pleasure ground down to short grass, I have made hay with it. The garden men mowed it & I made it with the stable people without any expense than giving them some ale [13] & it being fine weather it is excellent hay for the cows.

I have been obliged to pay the land tax [14] £55.8s for the Year '83 it being settled by the Commissioners of the Land Tax, but there will be a day of appeal the 21st of next month for the Year '84. I have not paid the money for the Highways nor shall I until the poor rates is settled, which will not be until the next Quarter Sessions. It was to have [been] tried last Quarter Sessions but the bench put it off. [At the end of this line Morice has written 'dated 26th April instead of July']
William Gould's year was up the first of June [15]
John Weeden's year was up the twenty fourth June

Henry Chroust's year was up the sixth of May
Robert Carter's year was up the twenty sixth of May
John Hankins's year is not up until the twentieth of December
Robert Carter's affair [16] is not settled. He says the last [torn] that Elizabeth Tanner swore to him is an imposition on him, that he would willing[ly] pay ten pounds. I have wrote to the Parish Overseers at Greenwich but I have not received any kind of an answer for which I don't [think] that they will accept of the ten pounds. Robert wishes not to leave his place but says that it is not in his power to pay any more and begs that Your Honour would be so kind as to give him your advice what he had best do in the affair.
I am Your Honour's Servant at Command
Will Bishop

Mrs Deale gives her duty to Your Honour. She is very well, is sorry to hear that you are not so well as you have been, desires to be remembered to Richard.

[On the back fold in Morice's hand] W. Bishop 20th August, answered 29th August

Notes

1. This is perhaps the dog that was reported as lost in the previous letter.
2. It seems very unlikely that John Weeden had suffered from small pox, this is a very serious illness and he would not have been walking about. It seems probable that he had suffered from chickenpox.
3. William Pitt is not mentioned subsequently.
4. For John Hankins' illness, see above, Letter 9, note 2.
5. Either an old member of staff or one who was now in Naples with Morice. He is never mentioned again and was not left anything in Morice's will so is probably the former.
6. For opodeldoc, see above, Letter 7 of 26 January, note 10. For Jully's sprain see Letter 9.
7. Another comment on an apparent question by Morice, who obviously retained a close interest in the estate.
8. For William Ball, see above Letter 8, note 13.
9. This is the third reference to John Bodenham for hats (see above, Letter 7, note 17).

10. These costs were indeed mentioned by Bishop on 23 February but he would not have received the draft to pay for them since it was not sent until 3 May, see annotation by Morice, written on the letter of 23 February.

11. Anne Morice, Humphrey's sister, died in 1777. This is the second reference to her (see above, Letter 7 of 26 January, note 6). This sum of money is underlined as was the coal money and Henry James's bill.

12. No letter of 8 June is now extant.

13. Ale would be expected by the harvesters in the normal course of events.

14. For land tax see Letter 10, note 11. For the poor rate still not being settled, see above, Letter 9 of 25 March, note 5.

15. The year for which servants were hired was obviously not from Michaelmas, but must have been ad hoc depending on circumstances. See 4 January when John Hankins was reported as having been hired for the year since he was satisfactory.

16. For this 'affair' of Robert Carter, see below, Letter 10 of 29 April, note 16. From the cryptic reference it seems likely that it was first mentioned in a letter which we no longer have.

1. Humphrey Morice painted by Pompeo Batoni in about 1762. (Wadsworth Atheneum Museum of Art, and Art Resource NY).

2. Group portrait of the Bull family, painted by Arthur Devis in about 1747. Levina, later Mrs Luther, is the little girl on the left. (Harris Museum and Art Gallery, Preston, Lancashire and the Bridgeman Art Library).

3. Humphrey Morice painted by Pompeo Batoni in about 1762. (Sir James and Lady Graham, Norton Conyers, Yorkshire).

4. Werrington House in Devon, the seat of the Morice family, in 1832. (Authors' collection).

5. Grove House, Chiswick, engraved in 1792. (Authors' collection).

Summer House   *Captⁿ Louth's*

6. Detail from Samuel Leigh's *Panorama of the River Thames*, 1830, showing the Grove estate, at that date belonging to 'Captain Louth' i.e. Robert Henry Lowth. (Local Studies Collection, Chiswick Library).

7. Gunnersbury House, the home of Princess Amelia, in about 1770. (Local Studies Collection, Chiswick Library).

8. Early nineteenth century watercolour of Corney House, the home of John Towneley, Morice's neighbour. (Gunnersbury Park Museum).

9. St Nicholas church and the village of Chiswick from Walter Harrison's *History of London*, 1775. (Authors' collection).

10. St Nicholas church, Chiswick in 1791. (Local Studies Collection, Chiswick Library).

Above: 11. Turnham Green in about 1790, probably showing the north-east corner, by Samuel Hieronymous Grimm. (Local Studies Collection, Chiswick Library).

Right: 12. Watercolour of a footman, by G. M. Woodward, about 1790. (Lewis Walpole Library, Yale University).

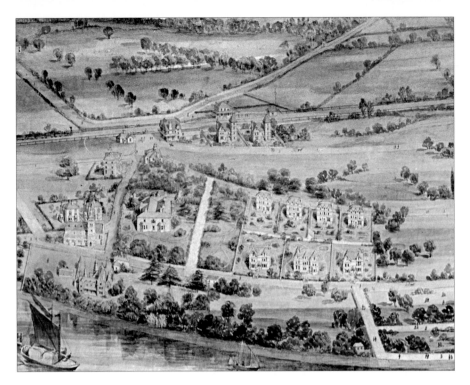

13. Detail showing the existing Grove House (left of centre) from an 1860s plan of how the remainder of the Grove Park area might be developed. (Local Studies Collection, Chiswick Library).

14. The tomb of the Paggen family in the burial ground in Wandsworth, where Humphrey Morice had intended to be buried. The arms on the tomb are those of the Paggen and Morice families. (Authors' collection).

Letter Thirteen

The Grove 20th August 1784

Honoured Sir

On the 5th August I received your letter dated 12th July [1] with the enclosed for John Vaughan. The draft that I meant which was returned, I had changed it with Mr Beniworth. He paid it to another man who sent it to Pall Mall for cash. The draft was refused on account its not being on stamp paper and there being no place abroad mentioned on the draft where it was drawn. The draft was returned to me [2].

On the morning of the 23rd June about half after two o'clock, Joseph Vickers see two men in the stable yard as he was in his lodge. As soon as Joseph appeared in sight of the men one of them leapt upon the wall by the gates. The other man was making off towards the necessary house. Joseph stepped up to him & told him that he had got him. The man immediately turn about and snapped a pistol at him. Joseph then snapped his pistol at the man. Their pistols both missed fire twice at each other. Joseph finding that his pistol would not go off, he then made for the lodge for his gun. In the meantime one of the men fired at him but missed him. The ball hit the wall about 3 yards from the lodge door. Joseph then catch up his gun and fired at the man who was on the wall as he could not see that who snapped his pistol at him at first nor can he tell where [whether] it was the man that was on the wall at first or the other that fired at him. He thinks he hit him as he heard the man fall down on the outside. Joseph was doubtful to open the gate in case there was more in the gang. He came and alarmed us in the house. This is the particulars as near as I can remember [3].

The old fence, that which is by the walk next the wall that goes from the little summer house to the great pond, is entirely rotten and broke down by the bull & the cows creeping under the new fence next the park. I have had a new rope put all along from post to post of the new fence to keep out the bull & cows from destroying the ivy that grows on the wall & the trees which are by the side of the walk.

A few days after I wrote my last letter to Your Honour the coach horse Smiler was taken ill. He refused his meat & water, his mouth was rather hot and dry, appeared to be feverish but no cough. I bled him, give him Marshes & the Jameses Powders [4] a few days, which he recovered is now in perfect health. The black mare Princess has got a humour [tumour] fell in to one of her hinder legs and under her belly which is swelled very much. I have bled her, give her physick and anointed the swelling with elder ointment [5], I hope she will soon get well as the swelling begins to go off.

The cockey & all the dogs are well. Flippant is brought to bed with two dog puppies & a bitch puppy.

Joseph Bowlden the farmer that we have the hay, straw & tares of would be glad to have a hundred pounds on account if it suits Your Honour. There is upwards of a hundred and fifty owing to him [6]. I had forgot in my last to tell you that Daniel Thompson [7] called at the Grove. He desired that I would give his duty to you, & that he was out of place.

Elizabeth Roberts is much as she was & John Hankins is rather weaker than he was some time back, I much doubt that it will end his days. Robert Carter has been ill with a pain in his stomach & a fever four or five days, is now got better than he was [8].

William Wapshott's Bill for Dogs [9]	£50.4s.4d
Joseph Beniworth's Bill for Raspings [10]	£16.10s.0d
His Bill for bran	£2.2s.5d
John Francis Bill	£7.19s.10d
Elizabeth Pulling's Bill	£4.12s.10d
John Maxwell's Bill	£2.4s.6d
Catherine Serman's Bills for a year [11]	£3.0s.3d
Lecturer [12]	£1.1s.0d

[In Morice's hand] 22nd Sept 1784 Paid by draft to W B £18.18s.6d [13]

On the 7th of this month I received Your Honour's letter dated the 25th of July with the drafts for £30, £31, £32, £33

Mr Cotton [14] called for the Parson's Afternoon Lecture & for two Christmas Boxes for himself.

John Weeden, Henry Chroust, William Gould all wants new boots against the horses come from grass, and Henry Chroust wants leather breeches.

I am Your Honour's Servant at Command

Will Bishop

Mrs Deale gives her duty to Your Honour. She is very well, is glad to hear that you are easier with the pains. Desires to be remembered to Richard.

Mr Gould the Maltster has left this neighbourhood, is gone to reside near Bagshot. What trifles we used to have off him we now have at the Strand on the Green of Mr Denyear [15].

[on the address panel Morice has written] W Bishop received 13th September, answered 21st [September]

Notes

1. Your letter dated 25 July: the dates of these letters rarely seem to agree with Morice's notes of letters sent, although they do sometimes. This may be due to the fact that not all the letters have survived.

2. This confusing passage seems to be saying that one of the money drafts sent by Morice had been refused payment because it was not properly drawn. What the final solution was, unless Bishop is saying that it had been replaced by Morice, is unclear.

3. This is the incident referred to in Letter 11.

4. It sounds as if the horse Smiler had suffered a return of his equine influenza, see Letter 6. For James's and Marshes powders, see above, note 4 of Letter 6.

5. Elder ointment was used to help reduce the swelling. It could be easily made from the common elderflower.

6. For the first reference to Bowlden, usually called Bolden, see Letter 4. He was paid the amount owing him; see Letters 15 and 17.

7. Daniel Thompson, another previous member of staff it seems, hinting that he would have welcomed an invitation to join the staff again, and might have been welcomed. This was not the case with all old staff, see Letter 7 above, note 5

8. Robert could have been suffering from a number of things, this was apparently a transient fever though.

9. Bills: William Wapshott's was probably for meat, he was a butcher; Elizabeth Pulling may be the Elizabeth Pullein who ran a grocer's shop

near St Nicholas church.

10. For raspings, see Letter 3, note 3.

11. This is the only reference to Catherine Serman, probably a tradeswoman, so that we do not know what she was being paid for.

12. The lecturer this year was a Revd Samuel Peshall, who was elected lecturer by the parishioners ('with the previous consent of the Vicar') on 18 July (*Chiswick Vestry Minutes, 1777–1817*, Local Studies Collection, Chiswick Library).

13. It is not clear what this draft was for; these figures do not add up to the amount of the draft.

14. Mr Cotton, the parish clerk, only wanted one Christmas box the year before. Perhaps he did not actually get that and so asked for two this year (see Letter 3, note 11, of 20 September 1783), and the lecture then was by the curate.

15. Bishop was apparently buying spent barley from the maltsters to feed horses. See Letter 17, note 8.

Letter Fourteen

The Grove 17th September 1784

Honoured Sir

A few days after I wrote my last letter to Your Honour John Hankins was so much worse that I was under the necessity of hiring a woman to look after him as a nurse [1]. He was so ill that he could not help himself or turn in his bed, he is now something better, is able to come downstairs.

At the same time there is not the least hopes of his ever getting the better of his complaint, although he may hold it out some months longer. I have all this time been without anyone in his room. As the horses has been at grass the greatest part of the time of his illness I thought there was not any necessity of getting a person in his room until such time as the horses came from grass again, when I should be glad to have one in his place as there is not the least hopes of his ever being able to work any more in the stables.

One William Seeger of Wandsworth, the Sexton, came to me to be paid for keeping your Honour's family vault clean [2]. He says that he has not been paid for the last four years past, that one Mr Simmonds always paid him before his decease, that he never has been paid since. I told him that I knew nothing of it, but that I would acquaint you of it. He says that he used to have four shillings per year for keeping the vault clean. I find by him that the vault is greatly out of repair, that part of the iron work is broke down and gone & part of the stone work tumbled down & wants repairing.

On Monday the 29th August Lieutenant King [3] of the Navy called here to enquire after Your Honour's health & desired his compliments to Your Honour.

Mr Saunders [4] have painted the stable yard gates & the outsides of the stable windows & the coping on the top of the house as the timber was decaying for want of painting and the wet penetrated through it. Mr Saunders wanted to paint all the outside work of all the house and premises but I told him that you would have nothing more to be done in your absence than really was necessary, so as to keep wind & water out.

I have had the good fortune to save all the second crop of hay without any rain. As we have had very warm weather this fortnight past I finished it last Tuesday.

Mr Webb Marratts Bill for Oats [5]

1783			
July 12th	To Oats - 25 quarters at 27s.6d		£34.7s.6d
	Lighterage		12s.6d
October 8th	To Oats - 25 quarters at 23s		£28.15s.0d
	Lighterage		12s.6d
December 17th	To Oats - 25 quarters at 23s.6d		£29.7s.6d
	Lighterage		12s.6d
1784			
February 16th	To Oats - 10 quarters at 24s.6d		£12.5s.0d
March 9th	To Oats - 15 quarters at 23s		£17.5s.0d

April 5th	To Oats - 40 quarters at 22s		£44.0s.0d
	Lighterage		£1.0s.0d
		[Total]	£168.17s.6d

[Written below in Morice's hand] 2 Nov 1784 Pd by a draft dated 26 Oct to W Marratt

John Holmes Bill [6] for a year   X   £3 17s 6d

[Against this Morice has written] X paid this through a draft to Jack Allan [7] 9 Nov 1784

Mr Bull came here on Friday the 3rd September. He told me that you have had the misfortune to have lost poor Tisby [8] which I am sorry to hear. Everything here is all much as it was when I wrote last. Princess is quite well of her complaint.

The trial came on yesterday at Hicks Hall [9] when it was compromised and settled at £330 per annum so that the half years poor rate is £24.15s.0d which is due Michaelmas 1783, so that Michaelmas 1784 there is two more half years poor rate due which is £49.10s.0d

[an X is written above the last money figure]

I am Your Honour's Servant at command

Will Bishop

[Following this Morice has written] X Paid two by a draft to W B for £49.10s.0d 2nd Nov 1784

Mrs Deale gives her duty to Your Honour. She is very well, desires to be remembered to Richard

[On the address panel Morice has written] W. Bishop received 7th October 1784, answered 2nd November. Webb Marrotts account

Notes

1. From this description of the treatment of John Hankins' illness it appears that Morice was willing for his staff, even relatively new ones, to be looked after as needed.

2. Morice apparently looked after the grave where his grandparents, mother and brother were buried. See illustration 14. See also below, Letter 16 of 4 February, note 5. Mr Simmonds may have been a previous senior member of Morice's staff.

3. Lieutenant King does not appear to be a relative of Morice.

4. Since Mr Saunders was probably Morice's land agent this probably means 'has had painted'.

5. For Mr Marratt see Letter 4 above, as the new supplier of oats mentioned there. The price of oats has been discussed earlier; Letter 8, note 3.

6. Mr Holmes has been paid before, but it was not specified what it was for then either; see Letter 3.

7. Morice's payment system seems rather complicated. We wonder why the bill for this relatively trivial amount was paid direct, and through a more senior member of staff, and not through Bishop as usual.

8. Tisby was perhaps a dog Morice had taken with him.

9. The marathon series of hearings over the previous year's poor rate thus ends here, about two weeks before the next year's rate was payable at Michaelmas, 25 September. For the poor rate see Letters 4, note 5 and 7, note 1. Hicks' Hall was where the Middlesex Quarter Sessions were held. It took its name from the previous Hicks Hall, pulled down in 1777 and named after Sir Baptist Hicks, who built it.

Letter Fifteen

The Grove 29th November 1784

Honoured Sir

On the 29th October I received your letter dated 5th October, on the 23rd November received Richard's letter [1] and on the 26th received your letter dated the 1st November with the draft for £49.10s. We have not seen or heard anything of Mr Row as yet, I am surprised at Row's behaviour [2].

I am sorry I did not understand that you meant to have Mr Marratt's bill sent you every time oats came in, but I have always had a bill sent when the oats was delivered in, of the quantity & the price as [it was? lost on the fold] against the bill. Oats has never been down so low as 16s 6d since you left England [3]. If they had I should have ordered in a quantity to have lasted a year. I look upon it that the corn factors are no greater gainers when oats are at a high price than they are at a low price for I believe that they always makes it a rule to have eighteen pence or two shilling per quarter profit let oats be at a high price or at a low price.

In a letter date 1st of July I received two drafts, one for £70, the other for £29.14s.6d for land tax, house tax, window tax, church rates, by ways & a small bill to Frances the smith [4].

The land tax for the year 1783 was obliged to be paid as it was settled by the Commissioners of the land tax before the poor's rate was settled. Mr Saunders has made an appeal to the Commissioners for the year 1784 which I suppose will be lowered now the poor rates are settled. The by ways was lowered from £12.6s.3d to £8.13s.3d as I would not pay it until the poor rate was settled [5].

I have not got one in John Hankins' place. I waited to hear from Your Honour first. I have now wrote to Mr Kerby to get me a weekly helper. There is not another half year's poor rate due until Lady Day next, I have had the money and paid up to Michaelmas 1783.

I am quite unhappy that I cannot get any account of what is become of James Bishop [6].

From 26th July 1782 to July 1783 [7]	Board wages	£256.10s.0d
	Garden Men	£137.0s.0d
	Poor rate & taxes	£128.2s.0d
	Servants wages	£64.18s.0d
	Bill Paid	£55.9s.0d
	Sundries	£38.19s.0d
	[Total]	£680.18s.0d

To December 1783	Board wages	£97.4s.0d
	Garden Men	£42.10s.0d
	Taxes	£5.16s.6d
	Servants wages	£12.0s.0d
	Bills paid	£44.14s.0d
	Sundries	£14.12s.8d
	[Total]	£216.17s.2d

To September 1784	Board wages	£174.12s.0d
	Garden men	£52.10s.0d
	Rates & Taxes	£118.14s.0d
	Servants	£35.14s.0d
	Bill Paid	£64.4s.6d
	Sundries	£28.18s.0d
	[Total]	£474 12s 6d

From 26th July 1782 to the 30th September 1784   Expended £1,372.7s.2d

I have but one draft left & about seven or eight pounds in cash. I have entered 4 coach horses & 6 saddle horses at the Stamp office [8]. Those that are not in use does not come under the account, nor the two cart horses. Our horses are all much as usual except the gray mare Lady Thigh, she has thrown out a spaven [9] on the off leg behind. The Cockey and all the dogs is well.

John Hankins is much as he was when I wrote last to Your Honour.

Mr Ockland [10] desired me to acquaint Your Honour that the gentleman of Chiswick has entered in to a voluntary subscription to prevent robberies in the parish of Chiswick, any gentleman may subscribe from two guineas to twenty.

Joseph Bolden's Account for a year [11]
Loads

36½ of Hay at £3.2s.0d per Load		£131.8s.0d
40½ of Wheat Straw at £1.7s.0d per Load		£54 13s 6d
9 of Oat Straw at £1.1s.0d per Load		£9.9s.0d
156 Bundles of Tares at a shilling per Bundle		£7.16s.0d
	[Total]	£203 6s 6d
	Received on Account	£100.0s.0d
	Due to him	£103.6s.6d

I have agreed with Mr Bolden for the ensuing year: Hay at £3.6s.0d per Load, Straw & Tares the same as [torn edge of page]

John Vaughan has made more than £10.2s.6d clear [of all?] expenses this year of walnuts & chestnuts [12].

Either on Wednesday or Thursday night last so[me] person or persons broke out & carried away 55 of the iron spikes belonging to the great [iron] gates at the bottom of the park near the great pond [13].

I am Your Honour's Servant at Command
Will Bishop

Mrs Deale gives her duty to Your Honour. She is very well, she has received the letter from Mr Spiers [14] to her satisfaction. Desires to be remembered to Richard.

Mr Game [15] called here on Sunday the 21st, he enquired after Your Honour's health, Mr Allan, Stracey & Richard. He is very well. I think that he seems to be greatly distressed, he has hinted to me that he should be very happy if he could but have an opportunity of serving his old master again.

[On the address panel Morice has written] W. Bishop received December 1784, answered 20th February 1785, with his accounts. H

Notes

1. Richard is referred to in every letter; he was almost certainly the son of Mrs Deale, but the letter seems to have been to a Mr Spiers, see note 14 below.
2. For Mr Row, see above, in Letter 4 of 30 October 1783, note 14. Unfortunately we have no idea what exactly Row had done but he was apparently dismissed for it, see Letter 16, 4 February 1785.
3. For the price of oats, see above, Letter 4 of 30 October, note 3. It does sound as if Morice was querying why Bishop was paying more for oats than when he was last in England.
4. For these bills see Letter 10, notes 11, 12, 13 and 14.
5. For Mr Saunders see note 1 in Letter 5. Settling these taxes was obviously a complicated affair since they were all tied together, being based on valuations of the same houses.
6. James Bishop was perhaps a relative of Will Bishop but he is not mentioned before or after.
7. There seems to be no regular accounting period. It is a pity that from these figures we cannot work out what the staff were actually paid, although since we do not know how many there were, any calculations would be guesswork. It does appear that Bishop may have been accounting for the 'garden men' although their wages haven't been mentioned before. The total is a lot of money, all of which Bishop had probably accounted for. The odd starting date of 26 July 1782 may well be when Morice left England and the board wages would begin.
8. Bishop was registering these horses and paying excise duty under

a new tax introduced in September 1784. For every horse of the kind described ten shillings had to be paid.

9. This spaven in Lady Thigh is mentioned in the next letter (see below note 2).

10. For Mr Ockland, sometimes spelled (correctly) as Auckland, see above, Letter 6, note 6. He was obviously involved in setting up this voluntary vigilante group, perhaps at the instigation of his employer the Duke of Devonshire. Such groups were common about this time. See illustration 19.

11. Mr Bolden had asked for money on account in August, see Letter 13.

12. For the previous year's crop see Letter 5, 30 November 1783, note 5.

13. Incident of stolen iron, refer to Letter 17 below. These incidents point out the need for the vigilante group, as does the burglary incident in Letter 13 of 20 August 1784.

14. We have no idea who was Mr Spiers was, or why he should be writing to Mrs Deale.

15.Game was obviously an ex-employee since he knew some of the staff (see above, pages 14-15).

Letter Sixteen

The Grove 4th February 1785

Honoured Sir

I have received two drafts from Mr Kerby one for £30, the other for £31 [1]. I am sorry to hear that Your Honour have been so ill. Jane Powers have had an inflammation fell in to one of her legs, she is now got about again. John

Hankins has been so very ill this month past that we expected every day to be his last. I think it impossible that he can hold it out much longer. His mother has been here this three week & she wishes to stay to see the last of him. The rest of us are all well except Elizabeth Roberts & she is still lame.

The gray mare Lady Thigh has thrown out a spaven. I have had her blistered, she is got better [2]. The rest of the horses are all much as usual. The Cockey and all the dogs is well. X Robert Carter wishes to have ten guineas advanced him on account [3]. [Between the lines Morice has written] X 14th Mar 1785 sent him £14.14s.

Last Tuesday the Duchess of Montrose [4] called here to inquire after Your Honour's health, desired her compliments & hopes that we shall hear by the next account that Your Honour is well.

Last Monday night we had a terrible high wind which blew down two of the large walnut trees in the park.

John Constable Churchwarden at Wandsworth has been here for two years annuity due at Christmas last £10.0s.0d [5].

The Surveyors of the Highways have been for money for the year ending at Michaelmas 1785. The same as last year £8.13s.3d [6].
[Under this Morice has written, with each part bracketed together]
14 Mar [May?] 1785, a draft to William Bishop to pay these.
The same as last year £8.13s.3d, Moses Hadley [7] £6.5s T[otal] £14.8s.3d.

Mr Ockland called for the money for the tithe of the hay [8] due at Christmas last £3.17s.6d.

William Wopshott [9] Collector of Window & House Tax called for half a years tax due at Michaelmas last: Window tax   £6.1s.6d
                                             House tax   £3.15s.0d
[Against Wopshott on the blank sheet facing the entry Morice has written]
14th Mar 1785 not paid told WB to pay it [and under house tax] a draft to [him] 14th March 1785 £9.6s.6d.

Mr Wopshott says that the reason those taxes is paid half yearly now is on account of the new Duty [10] being laid on, which took place at Michaelmas last & must be collected every half year. [After 'half year' Morice has written] These six [11] paid by a draft to WB for £28 14th Mar 1784

Bills sent in since Christmas last
Charles Blake Tinman a Bill	£2.13s.0d
Mathew Right Bricklayer a Bill	£6.9s.11½d
John Francis Smith 2 quarterly Bills	£2.15s.8d
Frances Gray Seeds Woman a Bill	£3.19s.3d
William Salter of Richmond a Bill	£9.15s.11d
John Jullion of Brentford a Bill	£2.5s.6d

[under this last line in Morice has written]   £27.19s.4d ------------£28
Joseph Hern of Hammersmith   a Bill   £16.17s.6d
[alongside on facing blank] Paid a draft 14 Mar 1785 to W Bishop inclosed
Frances Morgan Carpenter   a Bill   £13.9s.11/2d
[alongside on facing blank] Paid a draft 14 Mar 1785 enclosed to WB
Robert Richins of Richmond   a Bill   £33.3s.1d
[alongside on facing blank] Paid a draft 14 Mar 1785 enclosed to Mr [illegible]
William Curtis of Chiswick   a Bill   £16.11s.0d

[alongside on facing blank] Paid a draft 14 Mar enclosed to W Bishop
[all notes about payment in Morice's hand]

I sent yesterday to know how Mrs Phillips & all the dogs was. Mrs Phillips has been very poorly for some time, is now something better than she has been [12]. The dogs are all well.

Row [13] has not been at the Grove. What few things he had here are sent to him, he arrived in Town on the 12th December.
I am Your Honour's Servant at Command
Will Bishop

Mrs Deale give her kind duty to Your Honour. Hopes that your Honour and all with you is well. Desires to be remembered to Richard. She is very well.

There has been a putrid fever [14] ranged here for some time past & has carried off a great number of people round this neighbourhood [15].

[On address panel Morice has written] W Bishop received 3rd March, answered 14th enclosed draft. H

Notes

1. It is not clear what these drafts were for.
2. Bishop told Morice of this in the previous letter. A spavin is a bony swelling around a leg joint. They often develop in old age and can cause considerable pain when they develop. Blistering was not normally used to cure these; it is the name used when an irritant paste is applied to an area where there is an underlying tissue damage such as a sprain. The tissue reaction theoretically causes additional blood supply to the area which cures the damaged tissue. A mild blistering agent such as mustard was

sometimes used, or mercuric iodide which was more severe. Lady Thigh is noted in the next letter as better.

3. Presumably Robert Carter wanted this ten guinea advance to buy off the poor law officers from Greenwich.

4. Visit of Duchess of Montrose. This is her second visit in these letters, see Letter 4 of 30 October 1783, note 15.

5. If this annuity that the churchwarden of Wandsworth was asking for was for looking after Morice's family grave, this ten guineas is a lot more than the sexton claimed in September 1784, see Letter 14, note 2.

6. The surveyor (or surveyors) of the highways were appointed by the parish but the vestry records at this time do not say who they were. One may have been Thomas Dancer, who collected the Highway rate in April 1784, see Letter 10.

7. Mr Hadley is not mentioned before or after, so we do not know what he was supplying them with.

8. Mr Auckland was the receiver for the Duke of Devonshire in Chiswick. For tithes, see above, Letter 6, note 6.

9. Mr Wapshott was still a churchwarden in this year.

10. Bishop may mean that the house and window tax were assessed on the same form from 1784 and that this meant that they had to be paid half-yearly.

11. The six referred to are the first six in the column following.

12. For Mrs Phillips see also Letters 7 and 17.

13. Mr Row is referred to above in Letters 4 and 15. It sounds as if Row junior had been dismissed by Morice for whatever it was he had done and was now in England.

14. Putrid fever is typhus.

15.Deaths in the parish records: in view of Bishop's remark it is odd that for the period December to January in 1785 there was only one more burial recorded in Chiswick Parish church than in the same period in 1784 (sixteen as opposed to fifteen) and far fewer in February 1785 than in February 1784 (five as opposed to fifteen) so there is no sign of 'a great number' being carried off in 1785.

Letter Seventeen

The Grove 4th April 1785

Honoured Sir

On the 23rd March I received your letter with Mr Bolden's draft and three other drafts [1]. I am sorry to hear that Your Honour had the misfortune [to] fall backwards down stairs but I hope by this time you have quite recovered [from] the shock of the fall [2].

The gray mare Lady Thigh is quite sound of her lameness. The rest of the horses are all well. The Cockey & all the dogs is well.

It entirely slipped my memory when I wrote last to tell you that we lost 20 more of the iron spikes since we lost the 55 [3]. I was informed that a fisherman belonging to the Strand on the Green was taken up in Town on suspicion of stealing of iron as he had a large quantity on board his boat, such as green palisades, plough shares, harrow tines &c. I sent Joseph Vickers to Town to see if that any of the palisades belong to us but none of them proved to be ours.

Our coals being quite out I have ordered in five chaldron only for the present use as I found that coals was very dear at this time. I am [bottom third of page has been torn off]
In[words missing] W[words missing] F[words missing]

On Friday the 25th of March Elizabeth Roberts was taken ill with a complaint in her bowels attended with a fever. She on Saturday grew worse & continued so until last Saturday which carried her off about a quarter after two o'clock notwithstanding every necessary assistance was given her [4]. I have ordered her funeral with regard to the expenses as near as I can recollect to that of poor John Helston's [5].

On Saturday the 19th March Mr Coffen with Mr Hole & Sir John Chisetter [?Chichester] came to see the Grove [6]. A few days ago I called on Mrs Phillips. She gives her duty to Your Honour, is sorry to hear that you have been so ill. She is very poorly herself, the little dogs are all well.

It was very extraordinary of John Hankins' mother [7]. The day after I had sent my last letter to Your Honour she took it into her head to go home under pretense to fetch herself some clothes, but she has taken care not to return again notwithstanding she knew that everybody expected every day to be the last.

F[missing] … necessity of hiring a [bottom third of page torn off]

The Overseers of the poor has been for half a year's poor rates due Lady Day last - £24.15s.0d

[written under this line in Morice's hand] Paid by a draft to WB 3rd May 1785

It being an eighteen penny rate this year makes it a third more than the last half years that is paid.

Thomas Denyer's Bill [8] for Malt & Beans for the horses	£1.12s.3d
Barley for the fowls	£2.2s.0d
[Total]	£3.14s.3d

Mr Marratt's Bill for Oats

1784 September 13th 30 quarters at 23s.6d	£35.5s.0d
Lighterage	£0.15s.0d
December 14th 10 quarters at 22s	£11.0s.0d
1785 January 7th 30 quarters at 20s 6d	£30.15s.0d
Lighterage	£0.15s.0d
March 15th 30 quarters at 19s	£28.10s.0d
Lighterage	£0.15s.0d
[Total]	£107.15s.0d

[Written under this by Morice] Paid by a draft enclosed to Jack Allan 20th June 1785 [9]

[On address panel Morice has written] W Bishop received 1 May 1785, 10th May Marrats bill for 15 [sic] September 1784 to 15 March 1785. H

Notes

1. The draft for Mr Bolden was probably for the amount outstanding in November, see Letter 15.
2. Morice falling downstairs may have hastened his death some six months later.
3. For the previous theft of iron railing, see above, Letter 15 of 29 November, note 13.
4. Elizabeth Robert's final illness seems unlikely to have been related to her long-term lameness. It could have been typhus.
5. We know nothing of John Helston. He was not buried in Chiswick so he may have died while Bishop was still at Werrington. It is interesting that Bishop had been responsible for this burial too, another example of his ambiguous position. Elizabeth Roberts had been ailing for some time (see above, note 4).
6. We do not know who these people are. Chichester and Coffin are West Country names so they may well be friends from Morice's time in Werrington.
7. For John Hankins and his illness and his mother's presence at his sickbed, see above, Letter 16.
8. For a previous reference to buying malt, see Letter 13, note 15.
9. It does look as if Morice liked to see that Mr Marratt's bill was paid by himself or Allan rather than by Bishop. See note 5, Letter 14.

Letter Eighteen

[A single sheet, the last page of a letter. There is no date but Morice's note on address panel says received 19th May so probably sent late April or early May]

Mrs Deale gives her duty to Your Honour. She is very well. Desires to be remembered to Richard.

William Gould's year [1] will be up July 1st   £10.10s.0d
John Weeden year up May 24th   £10.10s.0d
Henry Chroust year up May 6th   £10.10s.0d
                                    [Total]   £31.10s.0d
[Under this Morice has written] Paid by a draft to WB May 14 [2]
13 June 1785   J. Vickers to July 1785   £7.16s
                                    [Total]   £53.6s [3]

Joseph Vickers has not been paid the money due to him the 24th of July last, two years account

I am Your Honour's Servant at Command
Will Bishop

[written under in hand of Morice is £2.2s, £2.12s and £1.12s with a partial sum of 16 underneath]

[On back fold in Morice's hand] W Bishop received 19th May

Notes

1. These are all stable lads who, if this represents their wages, as it presumably does, were thus paid ten guineas per year. This comes to four shillings a week, a reasonable wage for a stable lad.
2. If Morice received this letter on 19 May as he said in his note on the front then he cannot have sent a draft on 14 May.
3. Vickers was apparently owed two years' wages up to 24 July 1784, plus presumably his wages to the date of the letter. It appears that he was paid £7.16s. per year, a rather odd sum but not far from the £10 which was about what a porter might expect in 1785. The figure of £53.6s. may represent the total of £31.10s, (the wage bill for Bishop's three staff), plus Vickers' back-pay. This does not work out exactly, so we may be misunderstanding the situation completely.

Letter Nineteen

The Grove 1st September 1785

Honoured Sir

I am very sorry to acquaint you that I have lost poor Truelad. How it happened God knows, I cannot account for it. The dog was very well the over night at eight o'clock but in the morning he was found dead under the gray mare Lady Thigh's manger. I examined him thoroughly but could not find that he had received any hurt anywhere, neither was he in the least swelled in his body but lay as if he had bin asleep. Poor old Nero breaks very fast. I doubt he will not last much longer. The yard dog Toss has been lame in his shoulder but is now got better. The rest of the dogs are all well & the Cockey is well

The cart horse Whitefoot is still poorly, he don't get the better of it as I could wish. He don't care to eat anything but green meat such as grass or tares. I am rather inclined to think that he is in a state of decline by his being so long of his stomach & continues to lose his flesh gradually without the least symptom of any other complaint [1]. Junice I think gets rather worse in his wind. The rest of the horses are all much as usual.

I am now making the second crop of hay. We had two or three fine days when I began to mow the meadows but the weather the last 3 days past is very unfavourable [several illegible words - possibly scraped out] I am not sure whether I told Your Honour in my last letter [2] that I should want £14 to pay Goble for making this second crop of hay or not.

Robert Carter has been very poorly for some time with a complaint in his back & loins. He is now got brave again [3]. I have had a helper during Robert's illness.

Mr Bull was here last Sunday. I am sorry to hear that Your Honour is so poorly. I hope by the next account we shall hear that you are better.

The land tax [4] is now lowered down to £43.16s.0d which was due Lady Day last.

Joseph Benyworth's Bill for Raspings [5]	£16.4s.0d
His Bill for Bran	£0.12s.0d
William Wopshots Bill for Sheepheads [6]	£51.18s.8d
Elizabeth Pullins Bill	£4.3s.7d
John Maxwell [7] Bill for evening posts	£2.5s.6d
The Curate's Afternoon Lecture [8]	£1.1s.0d
Mr Cotton the Clerk's Christmas Box [9]	£0.5s.0d
[Morice has written against these entries] All these paid by drafts to WB 28 Sept 1785	
Ann Light [10] at Chiswick a Bill	£0.5s.1d

Mr Light, tailor, has been dead some time. His widow has now sent the bill in. I told her that I knew nothing of it, that I would acquaint Your Honour of it. The bill is for mending a coat & two waistcoats of yours in May & July in the year 1782

Mr Moffett [11], Overseer of the poor of Chiswick have been for half a year's poor rate due Michaelmas next. This half year is three shillings in the pound which brings it up to £49.0s.0d. The reason it being rose to 3 shillings in the pound this half year is owing to the expense the parish has been at in building & enlarging the workhouse at Turnham Green [12].

I changed the last draft that I received of Mr K[erby] [13] on the 9th of August.

I have been told that Thomas Wills is dead at St Stephens [14], that he give himself up to drinking of Spirit which shortened his days. In what circumstance he has died in, or how he has left his affairs, I have not heard.

I am Your Honour's Servant at Command

Will Bishop

Mrs Deale gives her duty to Your Honour. She is very well. Desires to be remembered to Richard. She is much happier in her new lodgings than she was at Weatherlys [15]. The ill treatment she received from Weatherly's wife from time to time that it made her life miserable & quite unhappy.

[On the address panel of the letter Morice has written] W Bishop with drafts September 1785

[The following text is from a fragment written on one side by Morice. This is even more shaky than usual, The fragment was folded into the letter]

[Side 1: in Morice's hand]

Mr W B	£43.16s.0d
Josiah Bennyworth	£16.16s.0d
W. Wasphott	£51.18s.8d
Mr W B	£8.0s.6d
Mr W B	£49.10s.0d
[Total]	£170.0s.6d

Paid 27 Sept 1785 [16]

[Side 2. In the hand of a correspondent] [17]

the lineal descent [torn]
William Molesworth is [torn]
property I have be [torn]
so as many years I [torn]
it on the other side [torn]
I beg my complaisance [torn]
and that this may fin [torn]
sincere wish of [torn
Sir
your m[torn]
servant

Lord Tylney died [torn]
pleurisy on his lung [torn]

Notes

1. Without further information it isn't possible to say what might have been the problem with Whitefoot. Perhaps he could not eat because of bad teeth although Bishop would almost certainly have been aware of that kind of trouble. Lack of further information means that we have no idea why the dog Truelad died. Perhaps in his case it was old age.
2. This reference to 'Goble' does not appear in the previous letters we have so that one or more of Bishop's letters must be missing. Goble was

presumably someone who had helped with the hay-making.

3. This could be many things, but perhaps could have been the passage of a kidney stone.

4. The reduction in the land tax had at last been achieved as a result of the interminable appeals, see Letters 10, notes 11, 12, 13, 14 and Letter 15, note 5.

5. For raspings see Letter 3, note 3.

6. Mr Wapshott was the butcher, see Letter 3, note 2.

7. John Maxwell was presumably the local postmaster. See also Letters 3 and 13.

8. The subscription for the curate's lecture was the same as the subscription for the previous year's lecture.

9. We do not know how much Mr Cotton was given for his Christmas box in previous years.

10. Ann Light has not been mentioned before.

11. Mr Moffett was selected as one of the six overseers of the poor in March 1785.

12. Chiswick Workhouse was built in 1725 and enlarged in 1785. In August 1785 the vestry meeting agreed to allow a Mr Thomas Hall to erect an additional building to the workhouse at a cost of £275 and although they agreed to pay him in two instalments in November and January, they obviously wanted to be sure to start getting the money in advance.

13. At least some drafts were obviously sent to Kerby, who then passed them on to Bishop.

14. Perhaps someone living in St Stephens by Launceston, near Werrington.

15. This is the only piece of evidence that Mrs Deale did not live at the Grove.

16. These calculations refer to the sums owed in the letter. They show a very careful man doing his own accounts and clerical work even if the handwriting is very shaky. The use of this small piece of paper torn from a letter also shows a man unwilling to waste the back of letters.

17. This fragment comes from a letter written to Morice, the handwriting is different to his, it is not at all shaky. It may refer to Morice's will, Sir John Molesworth (not William) was a distant cousin of Morice but he did not in fact leave him anything, although Morice's cousin Sir William Morice, from whom he had inherited Werrington, had left the Molesworths considerable property. Lord Tylney was a neighbour of Morice in Naples. In the Naples codicil to his will Morice requests that after his death the surgeon at Lord Tylney's house makes quite sure he is dead before burial. Tylney died in September 1784. Like Morice he had also been a friend of Sir Horace Mann.

Letter Twenty [1]

The Grove, 12th September 1785

Honoured Sir
On the 3rd I received Your Honour's letter dated the 8th August [2] with the four drafts.

On Monday night & all day Tuesday we had dreadful stormy weather The wind blew exceeding hard at south west which has blown down one of the great Arbbale [3] trees in the pleasure ground & the great thorn tree by Oronooko's paddock & a number of limbs in the park, & stripped one end of the roof of the shed in the back yard, and broke a great number of tiles which I have had repaired [several scraped out words follow]

Since I wrote my last the great bay mare Genny Cammil has had a humour fell in to one of her hind legs which was swollen very much. I have given her a dose of physick & she is a great deal better [4].

Last Monday two of the Greenwich Officers and old Tanner [5] came here to take up Robert Carter [6] for the expense of the two bastard children sworn to him some time back by Elizabeth Tanner, but they missed him. However they are determined to have him in case he does not pay down 20 pound.

The following is what Robert desired me to send you:

Honoured Sir
I beg pardon for troubling you again and for what I have been guilty of, and am sorry to impart that adversity obliges me to resume my former petition, for the Greenwich gentlemen are determined not to let me rest in peace

except I comply with their request, which is quite inconsistent to my ability at present as I have no more money than my present use requires. So in case I am taken Your Honour is sensible what must ensue or marry the girl which I am determined at all events never to acquiesce to. Am very thankful for what Your Honour have already done for me, and at this critical time it may be the means of preventing your unfortunate petitioner from utter ruin, so rest in hopes to experience still Your Honour's goodness that Sir you will be pleased to advance me one year's wages or twenty pounds on account to settle the affair & your petitioner as in duty bound will ever pray.

I am Sir Your Honour's Servant at Command
Will Bishop

[On the address panel is written] Sept 1785 W Bishop [7]

Notes

1. There are no notes about payments written on the address panel or the back of the letter as there usually are. Morice died on 18 October 1785 and so he may not have received the letter before he died. See also note 7 below.
2. Morice's letter of 8 August was presumably in answer to one of the missing letters.
3. An abballe or abele tree is a white poplar.
4. Genny (or Jenny) Cammile has been mentioned several times as being lame.
5. Tanner was perhaps the father of the Greenwich girl Elizabeth Tanner.
6. For Robert Carter's activities see also Letters 10, note 16; 12, note 16 and 16, note 3. He was obviously desperate to escape from the difficulty he was in. It is a pity that we do not know how Morice would have responded, although since he gave Carter the advance that he had requested before (Letter 16, note 3) he might well have responded positively.
7. This final note is not in Morice's hand, nor is there a figure '85' in red, which, as in note 1 above, may show that he never saw the letter. His always shaky hand was distinctly worse in the fragment with the previous letter (Letter 19, 1 September, see note 16).

2

The Life of Humphrey Morice

Humphrey Morice was born on 17 May 1723 and baptised three days later at St Dunstan-in-the-East in the City of London. His parents lived close by in Mincing Lane.

His father, another Humphrey Morice, was a London merchant and slave trader. He had moved to Mincing Lane in 1720 after the death of his first wife Judith, by whom he had five daughters. In 1722 he married Katherine, the daughter of Peter Paggen, another City merchant, of the Manor House, Wandsworth. Humphrey was their first child, followed a year later by a second son, Nicholas. Katherine's first marriage had been to William Hale, MP for St Albans, but he had died in 1717, leaving her with two sons. So Morice's early years would have been spent in a comfortable and prosperous household, with his own younger brother and his five older half-sisters and two older half-brothers. Presumably the family were quite close, as one of his half-brothers later married his half-sister Elizabeth.

Humphrey Morice senior had made a successful and lucrative career from exporting goods from Europe to Africa, filling his ships with African slaves which he then sold in the New World, and returning with a cargo of gold and other imports. He eventually owned a fleet of eight ships, most of them named after his wife and daughters, and he also held shares in other ships and insured cargoes. As a respected merchant in good financial standing, he was made a deputy governor of the Bank of England in 1725 and held the post of governor from 1727 to 1729. However after his sudden death in 1731 everything changed. The Bank of England discovered that their former governor had defrauded the bank of some £29,000, he had forged bills and had also embezzled trust funds left to his own daughters, leaving enormous debts. Litigation dragged on for many years and a final settlement was not reached until the 1770s.

Despite the family's straitened circumstances Morice was able to attend Trinity Hall, Cambridge, briefly, from 1740 to 1741, but he left without taking a degree. Whilst there he subscribed to the 1744 edition of Samuel Butler's *Hudibras*, listing himself as a Fellow Commoner of Trinity Hall. Whether this means he was actually still at the university in 1744 will probably never be known.

Morice's fortunes changed in 1750 when his second cousin, Sir William Morice, died without issue. Sir William's baronetcy became extinct, but the family seat at Werrington in Devon, along with most of his other estates and his picture collection, passed to Morice as the next heir. The estates included two pocket boroughs, Launceston and Newport, each returning two members to the House of Commons. Morice's father had held one of the Newport seats from 1713 until 1722, and Morice now stepped into Sir William's shoes as one of the members for Launceston, at a by-election held in 1750. He held this seat until he finally resigned from Parliament in 1780.

In the eighteenth century Members of Parliament did not receive a salary, but a seat in the House of Commons conveyed status, influence and the opportunity to be appointed to some lucrative sinecures. Morice supported the Whig Duke of Newcastle in 1757 and was rewarded with the post of Clerk Comptroller of the Board of Green Cloth (the Board of Green Cloth audited the accounts of the Royal Household), which he held from 1757 to 1761. When Newcastle deprived him of this post Morice transferred his allegiance to the Earl of Bute, who formed a Tory administration in May 1762. Morice was given the coveted post of Comptroller of the Royal Household in December 1762, and sworn in as a member of the Privy Council in January 1763. There were moves to take the comptrollership from him, but he refused to give it up until he was able to exchange it for the office of Lord Warden of the Stannaries in June 1763, after Bute had been replaced by the Whig administration of George Grenville. This post he retained until ousted by the Fox–North coalition in the latter part of 1783.

In 1768 Morice asked for an office for life (unfortunately what office it was is not recorded) but this was refused by the king. In 1771 he was chosen as recorder of Launceston and held this post until he resigned it in 1782 after making his will and leaving for Italy. In 1772 he asked for the 'red ribbon' (i.e. to be made a Knight of the Order of the Bath) but the then prime minister, Lord North (a Tory), explained that the king felt that he had to give the next vacancy in the Order to Sir George Macartney, a diplomat.[1] Co-incidentally Sir George, by then Earl Macartney, later rented Corney house in Chiswick, near the Chiswick estate that Morice was about to buy.

With four parliamentary seats at his command, Morice disposed of considerable political patronage, and was usually able to accommodate candidates suggested by the government of the day, while also fitting in his own close associates such as Richard Bennett, Richard Bull and Peter Burrell, and retaining one of the Launceston seats for himself. He consistently supported the government of the day and voted for them, but he is not known to have ever spoken in any debate in the House. Had he been a man of more presence and authority he might well have become an important man in the government but this does not seem to have happened. Charles James Fox, writing to the Earl of Bute in November 1762 about the possibility of giving the comptrollership of the Royal Household to Morice, wrote that 'his character has a ridicule, to say nothing more, belonging to it; it will certainly lower the dignity of the place'. There is also a description of him at the election in 1754: 'Little Morice prattles very prettily in his own behalf, and is as peevishly well bred at an election as he is at a whist table when he looses a rubber', which probably had a grain of truth in it despite being written by the candidate who was heavily defeated by Morice's nominees. The *Public Ledger* wrote about Morice in 1779 that 'he affects to hate the House of Commons' and in fact he sold the Werrington estate to the Duke of Northumberland in 1775 together with his electoral influence in Launceston and Newport, writing that 'the trouble of it, not to say anything of the expense, is more than Mr Morice can bear with a constitution much impaired by gout'. However, he did remain a Member of Parliament until 1780.

Morice may have been somewhat insignificant as a politician but he was still respected as a man of business. Cavaliere Giulio Mozzi, a member of one of the ancient noble families of Florence, whom Morice had probably met when he was in Italy, asked him to act as his English representative in a complicated legal case. Mozzi had become friendly with the widowed Countess of Orford (Horace Walpole's sister in law), who had also spent some time in Italy, and when she died in January 1781 she left her entire estate to Mozzi. The will was disputed by her son, the 3rd Earl of Orford, on the grounds that some of her estate was family property and not hers to leave to others. Morice was not a lawyer but Mozzi obviously felt that he was a sensible man of business who would be able to sort out the complex legal problems. Morice and Horace Walpole tried to arbitrate between the two sides, although Morice had to withdraw from the affair before the will was eventually proved in June 1784, with Mozzzi as the sole legatee.

Sadly none of Morice's account books or estate papers survive, but he was a wealthy man with a large number of properties and investments to keep track of. He appears to have done his own accounts as there are careful notes in his own writing on most of the letters written to him from the Grove, as to what was owed and what drafts of money he had despatched to Will Bishop; sometimes he queried the cost of an item or why a bill was more than they had paid for the same item the previous year. In some cases his sums are written beside the items on the letters or on separate slips of paper.[2] The arithmetic does not always seem very accurate but that could be because there were other items involved which are not specifically mentioned in the letters. The annual payment of £600 that he left in his will for the upkeep of the animals after his death seems to have been carefully calculated, based on the actual costs of running the Grove in the last few years of his ownership of the estate.[3]

Before he retired from Parliament Morice had bought himself a country estate within easy reach of Westminster. In 1776 he purchased the Grove estate in Chiswick, an eighteenth-century house with pleasure grounds which had been laid out for the Earl of Grantham, a previous owner, and an extensive park, in all amounting to about 86 acres. According to Daniel Lysons[4], Morice made 'considerable additions to the house and built a large riding-house with excellent stables for thirty horses'. It has been suggested the Grove was his favourite home but despite this, if indeed that was so, he did not spend all that much time there, because he was frequently away from London seeking treatment for his health – he suffered from chronic gout, as had his father before him. He also had other health problems: writing to a cousin from Naples in December 1768 he described 'the frequent return of the old complaint in my breast which I have been subject to ever since I was a child, which brought me almost to death's door, and for which I went abroad eight years ago'.[5] He visited spa in Germany and also Bath to take the waters, and later tried 'some German mud-baths', as Horace Walpole wrote to a friend.[6] On several occasions he sought the warmer climate of Italy, living mainly in Naples, where he rented a villa. References in letters of the time show that he was in Italy in 1760–1, in 1762, in 1768–9, in 1779–80 and finally he spent the last few years of his life there from mid 1782 to his death in October 1785. When he wrote the March 1784 codicil to his will he had a house in the elegant and fashionable seaside suburb of Naples called Chiaia.

However, Morice did spend some of his time at the Grove and took part in the life of the area. It is not known if he attended the parish church, whose south aisle was added the year after he came to Chiswick, but he supported local good causes – his name appears regularly in the list of subscribers to the charity school for poor children run by the church. He usually gave two guineas a year, whereas the most generous subscriber, the Duke of Devonshire, gave four guineas, but most other subscribers only gave one guinea or ten shillings and sixpence.[7] He also contributed to the church's afternoon lectures and the parish clerk's Christmas box, and in his will he left £100 to the poor of Chiswick.

Morice did not allow his health problems to prevent him from having a busy social life. He is mentioned many times in Horace Walpole's letters, as they evidently moved in the same social circles. When Morice first went to Italy in 1760 Walpole wrote to his friend Sir Horatio Mann, the British Resident in Florence, recommending Morice to him, and when Morice arrived, Mann reported, 'We soon grew intimate and as yet, though the second day, have talked of nothing or of anybody but you and Mr Chute, upon whose accounts I shall take to him violently.'[8] John Chute, another lifelong sufferer from gout, was a mutual friend of both of them. He was an architect and art connoisseur who had helped Walpole create his Gothic extravaganza at Strawberry Hill. On another occasion Walpole described a party in 1779 given by Princess Amelia, who lived nearby at Gunnersbury House and was also acquainted with Morice. Various peers and lords and ladies were there and Morice had also been invited, and turned up 'looking dreadfully ill'.[9] Walpole 'called upon' Morice at Chiswick in June 1781, though unfortunately there is no letter describing this visit, and dined with him and John Towneley (who lived nearby at Corney House) at the Grove on 19 July 1782, shortly before Morice left England for the last time. He was not at all well then: Walpole reported to one of his correspondents that Morice had totally lost the use of his legs and feet.[10] When Morice visited Mann in Florence in October 1783 Mann reported to Walpole that he was shocked to see that Morice was using crutches, but he dined with Mann 'en famille' several times and the next time was able to walk to his house.[11] Mann also took him to the theatre to hear 'the delightful Marchesi'. Perhaps Morice's problem with his legs, whether gout or something else, was what caused him to fall backwards down the stairs in Naples early in 1785; Will Bishop sent his commiserations in his next letter,[12] and in fact most of his letters included a note from himself or from Mrs Deale that they were sorry to hear that Morice had been ill.

It seems that Morice was able to keep cheerful despite his health problem; Walpole recorded in November 1784 that he had heard that 'Mr Morice is better, and as he always is, whether better or worse, in good spirits'.[13] Morice was obviously valued as a companion, a good person to have at a party – one example of this is an invitation couched in the form of a petition which is in the Swinburne papers in the Northumberland Archives.[14] A group were assembled at Ampthill Park, the seat of the Earl of Upper Ossory in Bedfordshire, and petitioned Morice to join them there for his 'agreeable cheerful company'. They said they were confident that he would be willing to do this because of his great humanity, 'even to the brute creation'. Perhaps this was a joking reference to his love of animals which must have been common knowledge to his friends. This 'petition' was signed by the hosts, the Earl and Countess of Upper Ossory and one of their daughters, as well as the Duke of Bedford and his younger son amongst others. This undated document must have been written not long before Morice left England for the last time in mid-1782, since the daughter of the Earl and Countess was only born in 1774 and her signature on the document is very neat and careful. It seems clear that Morice was a popular member of his circle of friends. The Bull family for example were very long-term friends, Richard perhaps from the 1740s when they were both at Cambridge, or at least from 1756 when he first became one of Morice's MPs. He was a witness to Morice's purchase of the Grove, a mark of respect.[15] Morice was a frequent guest at Richard Bull's house, North Court, in the Isle of Wight.[16] In his will Morice left generous annuities to Richard Bull, and to his two younger daughters Elizabeth and Catherine, while leaving the Grove to Bull's step-daughter Mrs Levina Luther, with remainder to Elizabeth and Catherine. Levina's brother Richard Henry Alexander Bennett, who married Elizabeth Amelia Burrell in 1766, was also part of the family circle. Morice's executor, the eminent lawyer William Burrell, was Elizabeth Amelia's uncle, and his other executor, John Claxton, was also a relative, being a connection of Morice's father's first wife.

Morice was generous to family, friends and servants, and there were several charitable bequests of £100 each in his will, to the poor of the parishes with which he was connected, Chiswick, Wood Walton and Wandsworth, and to the Lying In Hospital for Unmarried Women, the Small Pox Hospital and the Foundling Hospital. He was presumably also a supporter of the Lock Hospital for the treatment of venereal diseases as Will Bishop was able to find a signed letter of recommendation when he needed to send one of the staff there for treatment.[17] Morice was associated with the Foundling Hospital, which had been founded in the 1740s to rescue babies who had been abandoned or could not be supported by their parents. In 1755 he (together with many others) was called to the annual meeting of the governors and guardians of the hospital as Humphrey Morice of Berkeley Square, so he must have already been a subscriber to the hospital. Perhaps his interest had been partly aroused by the hospital's art collection; artists were encouraged to donate paintings and these were then put on display to help raise money for the hospital's running costs, making the building in effect the country's first public art galley. Morice was also generous to individuals: a letter to him from the well-known actress Kitty Clive in December 1761 acknowledged his 'great goodness to poor Mrs Kemp', to whom he had sent a gift of money in her distress; when Mrs Clive discussed this with a mutual friend he said 'it was like you'.[18] When one of his servants got into trouble for apparently fathering two bastard children and needed £10 to buy off the overseers from Greenwich, who would otherwise have 'taken him up', Morice sent him fourteen guineas to help him out of his difficulties.[19] In his will Morice left £500 to John Allan junior, probably the son of his servant John Allan, to set himself up in business after his apprenticeship was completed, and annuities to another young apprentice and to his godson Henry Kent. There were also gifts of £100 each to Charlotte and Hannah Allan, presumably also relatives of John Allan. His servants were well looked after: medicine was bought for them when they were ill and they were nursed at the Grove if they could not work, and funeral costs were paid if they died. Morice's will established annuities for at least eight servants and also several young people who were the dependants of his servants, and stipulated that all the servants could stay on in his house on board wages for three months after his death. The servants who were with him in Naples were to have all their living expenses paid plus the cost of travel so that they did not need to leave Italy until the weather was right for the journey back to England. 'I mean for them to continue in the house I inhabit at Chiaya 'till it is a proper season for them to return to England so as for them to avoid taking that journey during the extremes of winter or summer according to the time I may happen to die.' This considerate provision was written in the second codicil to his will.[20]

One of the great interests in Morice's life was paintings, and his art collection was much admired. He had inherited two paintings from his father, who died when he was only a boy, and then at least another twenty-four from his second cousin, Sir William Morice, who died in 1750, leaving Morice as his heir. Sir William had bought at least two of his paintings from Gunnersbury House, presumably when the contents of the house were sold at the death of one of the earlier eighteenth-century owners before Princess Amelia bought the house in 1761 – so these pictures had made a round trip from Gunnersbury to the family estate at Werrington in Devon and then later back to Chiswick. Subsequently Morice added to his collection by both buying and commissioning pictures. When he was in Italy in 1762 he took the opportunity to purchase a painting of *Diana and Cupid* from the celebrated artist Pompeo Batoni. Batoni was well known as a portrait painter of British aristocrats on the Grand Tour and Morice commissioned him to paint his portrait with three of his dogs.[21] Towards the end of his life he also inherited five paintings and a generous annuity of £1,500 from a relative, Lady Brown. Horace Walpole included a list of Morice's paintings in his *Journal*,[22] adding comments on some of them such as 'a most beautiful sea piece' against a painting by Claude Lorrain, or in less complimentary tones noting that two portraits of Elizabeth of York and of Henry VIII were bad copies. However, two of Morice's paintings by Salvator Rosa were much admired, and Lord Ashburnham, who bought Morice's art collection for the large sum of £4,000 after his death, was particularly interested in these. He had written to Morice's close friend Richard Bull in 1787, asking if he could see one of the Rosa works. Bull was obviously regarded as someone who could organise this since by then his step-daughter Levina Luther had inherited Morice's house the Grove. Richard Bull later wrote to Lord Ashburnham listing the pictures and their provenance, and where he knew them, the prices Morice had paid for them. Bull obviously knew the collection well.[23]

There were two aspects of Humphrey Morice's life that may have caused him to be looked at askance. The first and probably the major one was that he was almost certainly a homosexual. By the middle of the eighteenth century this was not regarded as tolerantly as it had been earlier in the century. Homosexuals were commonly accepted socially, but tended to be excluded from real political power. This may have been what happened with Morice, if he was indeed a homosexual. In fact, as sometimes happened to gay men at this time, he was the subject of attempted blackmail by three men in 1759. The men sent threatening letters to Morice, intending to extort money from him. The letters contained very thinly veiled accusations that Morice was a practising homosexual. Morice kept the men in play until he had sufficient evidence of conspiracy against them, and then caused them to be arrested. The men were found guilty of the conspiracy and sent to prison. Morice gave evidence that he had received and replied to letters from them.[24] After the case had been settled Morice decided to travel abroad; his health had probably suffered from the stress of the case, and he may also have wanted to allow the scandal to be forgotten before he again appeared in society circles.

The second reason why Morice was considered rather odd was that he was a great animal lover in a period when keeping animals that could no longer work was regarded as rather unusual. He was described by the dramatist George Colman the younger as 'thought to be, for more reasons than one, a *very* peculiar person'. Colman wrote that he remembered visiting the Grove as a boy with a relation, a lawyer, who was there on business. On entering the courtyard Colman described being 'assailed by a very numerous pack of curs in full cry', possibly exaggerating for effect. He went on to say that 'this was occasioned by Mr Morice's humanity towards animals: all the stray mongrels which happened to follow him in London he sent down to this villa where they were petted and pampered. He had a mare in his stables called "Curious" who, though attended and fed with the greatest care, was almost a skeleton, from old age, being turned of thirty'. Colman went on to say that many of Morice's horses enjoyed an idle existence, no longer expected to work but just allowed to enjoy the pasture of the estate. Interestingly an inventory of the Chiswick House estate in 1811 reveals that the Duke of Devonshire also kept a number of aged, blind and worn out horses in his stables.[25] Morice's concern for animals is shown in the letters themselves, which are very largely taken up by reports of the health of the various animals who are all mentioned by name, with details of their illnesses and occasionally their deaths. The fact that Will Bishop described to his employer the details of the 'sad misfortune [that] happened to one of Philis's young pups that was born since you left England'[26] seems to show that he knew Morice would want to know about this, and would be sorry to hear of the puppy's death. The puppy was chased by the other dogs, ran under the wheel of a cart and was killed on the spot.

Morice was aware of how other people might view this aspect of his character so when he made his will he decided to put his provisions for the future care of his animals in a letter to his executors rather than in the will itself. This letter left an annuity of £600 a year from his estates in Devon & Cornwall to pay for 'the maintenance of the horses and dogs I leave behind me and for the expense of servants to look after them besides Will Bishop the groom. He is I am persuaded very honest & will not let bills be brought in for any oats hay straw or tares more than have really been had'. As the animals reached the ends of their natural lives and died, the money left unspent from the annual £600 was to be returned to Mrs Luther, Morice's heir. He wrote that he could have included this provision in his will but that he 'thought it better to make my intentions known to you by a private Letter as their being mentioned in my Will would perhaps be ridiculed after my death, and although I should be ignorant of it and of course not care about it, yet the friends I leave behind me might not like to hear it'.[27] Morice obviously had faith in Mrs Luther's sympathy with his views about the animals.

Morice made his will just before he left England for the last time in July 1782. The will was signed and witnessed on 24 July. He probably left immediately after this since board wages for the servants left at the Grove started on 26 July that year.[28]

Morice was a very wealthy man in terms of both investments and property, so his will is long and complicated and is supplemented by the letter about the animals and a codicil written in March 1784 relating to his effects in Naples.[29] He appointed William Burrell and John Claxton, both lawyers and distant relatives, as his executors, leaving them £1,000 each for their trouble as well as a repeating watch each. As he wrote to Burrell at the end of the letter about the animals, 'I hope the Trust will not be a troublesome one to you – except just at first. Pray excuse it. When you receive this I shall be no more, but at the time of writing it am my dear Sir most sincerely yours, H Morice.' He instructed his executors to sell all his bank stock, East India stock and other financial investments, and his estates at Chipstead and Merstham in Surrey, at Wood Walton in Huntingdon and his London house in Dover Street. This money was to be used to pay the numerous legacies to friends and also charitable bequests. His estate at the Grove together with the family portraits and the furniture therein was left to the use of Mrs Levina Luther, the step-daughter of his great friend Richard Bull, and after her death to the use of her step-sisters, Elizabeth and Catherine Bull, who were in effect his residual legatees. Lady Mary Duncan wrote to the Bull sisters at the request of their father telling them of the good fortune of themselves and their father from Morice's will. She added at the end that when they got their inheritance it would amount to about £100,000 each, a very large sum indeed in the late eighteenth century, and possibly a somewhat exaggerated estimate. Lord Camelford, a friend of both the Bulls and Morice, also wrote to congratulate them on their good fortune, adding that he thought Mrs Luther, at the Grove, would be a good neighbour to himself. Camelford lived in Persham Lodge, Richmond, so it was not as a near neighbour.[30]

Morice also left a large number of annuities to friends, relatives such as Dame Jane Reeve and her three daughters, who were connections on his mother's side of the family, and to current and former servants, some charged upon plantations in Jamaica and others on the rents from his manors in Devon and Cornwall. He made generous provision for his servants and his animals, and he left his clothes and personal effects to his valet as was the normal practice, but also included one of his repeating watches, his diamond shoe- and knee-buckles and gold-headed canes. Perhaps he had a special relationship with his valet Richard Deale: in the letter of October 1782 attached to his will he recorded that 'his attention & fidelity increases every day & sorry I am to say he is the only servant I ever had who seem'd sensible of good treatment & did not behave ungratefully'.[31] However from the codicil written in March 1784 it appears that he had taken on a new *valet-de-chambre*, perhaps the Giovanni

Bruscogloni who was left over twice as much money as the other servants in Naples. He made Richard Deale one of his two executors in Naples to oversee the winding-up of his affairs there.

In his will of July 1782, Morice asked for his body to be 'interred in a private manner in the Vault in the Burying Ground of Wandsworth Hill wherein my mother and other relations are buried'. This vault is the splendid monument to the Paggen family of Wandsworth Manor House, Morice's maternal grandparents, in the Huguenot Burial Ground in East Hill, Wandsworth.[32] However, in a codicil to his will written in Naples on 14 March 1784, when Morice possibly faced the fact that he might never return to England, he wrote, 'I desire to be buried at Naples if I die there, and in a leaden coffin if such a thing is to be had. Just before it is soldered I request the surgeon … may take out my heart or perform some other operation to ascertain my being really dead.'

Humphrey Morice died in Naples on 18 October 1785 and is buried there, but the site of his grave is not known.

Illustrations

15. Detail from John Rocque's *Map of the County of Middlesex*, about 1755. (Local Studies Collection, Chiswick Library).

16. View of Chiswick across the fields, by William Hogarth, mid-eighteenth century. (Authors' collection).

17. Chiswick from the river, by Peter Brookes, 1750. (Authors' collection).

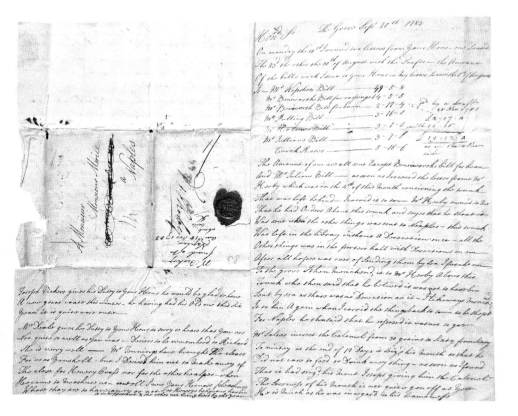

Above: 18. Letter 3 of 20 September 1783. (Local Studies Collection, Chiswick Library).

Right: 19. Poster produced by the Chiswick Association for Prosecuting Thieves, 1799. (Local Studies Collection, Chiswick Library).

Chiswick Affociation,

For Profecuting *Thieves* and *Felons*, &c.

WHEREAS Mr. *THOMAS DANCER*, of *Little-Sutton*, a Member of this Society, hath lately been ROBBED of a large Quantity of

Purple Brocoli Plants,

And *ROBERT NICHOLS*, one of the Offenders, a labouring Gardener, who Works for Mrs. *HAMET*. near *Kew-Bridge*, hath been Convicted of Stealing the fame, before *NICHOLAS BOND*, *Efq*. and others, his Majefty's Juftices of the Peace, on MONDAY, the 19th Inftant, at the Office, at *Kew-Bridge*; and the faid Mr. *DANCER*, is bound over to Profecute one *WILLIAM SAUNDERS* for receiving the fame, at the next Goal delivery for the County of *Middlefex*. And as *ROBERT SUMPTER* ftands charged upon Oath of being concerned as an Accomplice with the faid convicted *ROBERT NICHOLS*, in the faid Theft, but hath abfconded and fled from Juftice,---Now this Society promifes to pay a REWARD of

FORTY SHILLINGS,

To any Perfon or Perfons who will Apprehend the faid *ROBERT SUMPTER*, or give Notice to the faid Mr. *DANCER*, fo that he may be brought to Juftice, to be paid on Conviction by me

JAMES ARMSTRONG,
TREASURER.

Auguft 29, 1799.   Turnham-Green.

N. B. As a further REWARD, I promife to pay

Two Guineas,

On Conviction, as aforefaid, to any Perfon or Perfons who will Apprehend or caufe to be Apprehended, the faid *ROBERT SUMPTER*; he is upwards of 40 Years of Age, rather ftout made, is well known in the Vicinity of *Old-Brentford*, did Work for me, and is fuppofed to be now at Harveft Work.

THOMAS DANCER.

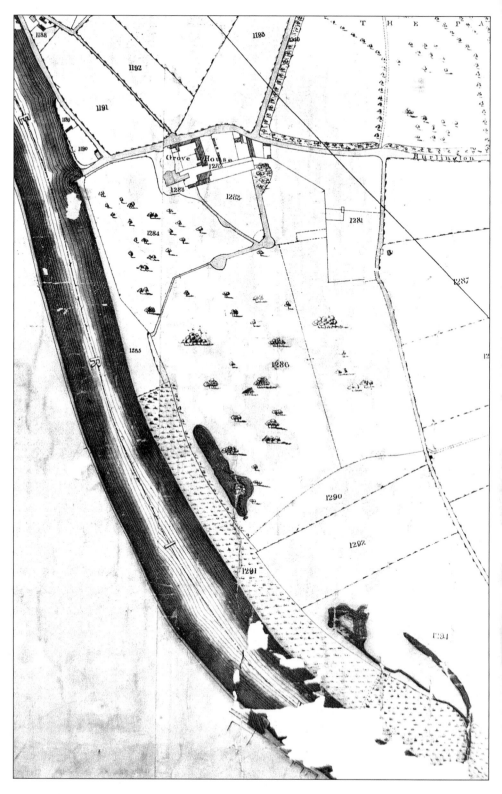

20. Detail showing the Grove estate from the 1847 tithe map of the parish of Chiswick. (Local Studies Collection, Chiswick Library).

Within the lithograph (left margin):

WROUGHT-IRON
ENTRANCE GATES
GROVE-PARK
CHISWICK
LONDON. W.

INCH—SCALE.

Measured, drawn & lithographed by
Thos: Garratt—May & Nov 1884.

21. Lithograph from a drawing of the entrance gates to Grove House, by Thomas Garratt, 1884. (Local Studies Collection, Chiswick Library).

22. The entrance gates to Grove House in 1905. (Local Studies Collection, Chiswick Library).

23. Early twentieth-century view of the gardens at Grove House, looking south. (Local Studies Collection Chiswick Library).

24. Early twentieth-century view of the west front of Grove House and the gardens, looking north-east (Local Studies Collection, Chiswick Library).

25. Early twentieth-century view of the gardens and outbuildings of Grove House. (Local Studies Collection, Chiswick Library).

26. Early twentieth-century view of the south side of Grove House. (Local Studies Collection, Chiswick Library).

27. The north front of Grove House in about 1923. (Local Studies Collection, Chiswick Library).

28. 1923 photograph of the drawing-room fireplace from Grove House, until recently on display as part of the 'Quinn Room' at the Huntington Museum and Art Gallery in California. (Local Studies Collection, Chiswick Library).

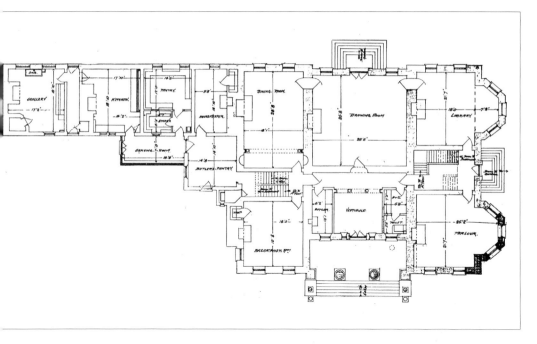

29. Plan of the ground floor of Grove House showing a possible extension, drawn by Charles Edward Hodge in 1889. (Val Bott Collection).

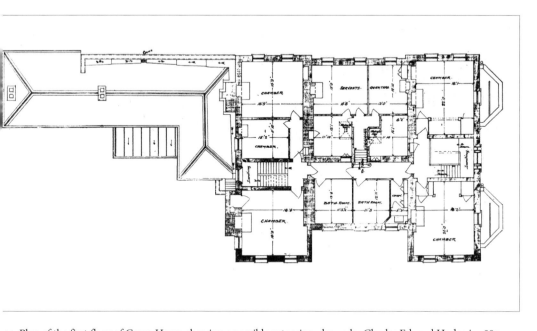

30. Plan of the first floor of Grove House showing a possible extension, drawn by Charles Edward Hodge in 1889. (Val Bott Collection).

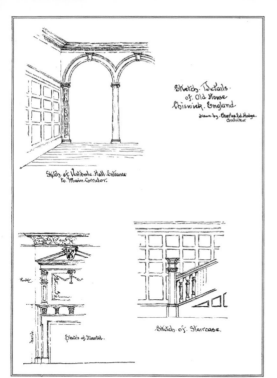

Left: 31. Sketches of details of the interior of Grove House by Charles Edward Hodge in 1889. (Val Bott Collection).

Above: 32. The drawing-room at Grove House *c*. 1928, just before demolition. (Local Studies Collection, Chiswick Library).

33. The back wall of the drawing-room at Grove House *c*. 1929, just before the house was demolished. Some of the new houses being built in its grounds can be seen through the windows. (Local Studies Collection, Chiswick Library).

3

The Grove Estate from the Beginning to 1775

The Grove house estate in the parish of Chiswick first enters history in the early fifteenth century with an entry in the Close Rolls. This was to the effect that Thomas Holgill acquired from the agents of John atte Wood the property known as the 'Grove' Sutton and Strand in the parish of Chiswick. It was thus already not just a small holding of land, but a holding in several parts of the parish. It may indeed have existed as a unit as early as 1202.[1] By 1597, an estate of 150 acres known as Grove Farm was being leased from St Pauls, the owners of the manor, by one Anthony Barker. The Barkers, who were originally from Sonning in Berkshire, may have been in Chiswick by 1537. They owned the land until the mid-eighteenth century. Their main house was known as Grove House by at least 1658.[2]

Succeeding members of the Barker family took an active part in parish affairs in Chiswick and as lawyers of the Middle Temple. They also continued to enlarge their estate.[3] By the time of Scorie Barker (named from his maternal grandmother's family), the estate had reached its maximum size in the care of the Barkers. Scorie was the most prominent of the Barkers of the Grove; he served as MP for Wallingford (the Barker family seat in Berkshire) from 1679–82 and then Middlesex from 1705–10. Scorie died in 1713 and was buried in Chiswick. He was succeeded by his son Henry, who was the last of the Barkers in Chiswick. Henry stood unsuccessfully for Parliament several times and continued to play a full part in the parish.

When Henry Barker died in 1745 he did not leave his Chiswick estate to his sons but left it to trustees, who conveyed part of the land to his cousin Henry Barker of Wallingford and sold the rest to the Duke of Devonshire, owner of Chiswick House. The reason for the disposal of the Chiswick estate by Barker was probably because soon after succeeding his father to the estates and house he was mortgaging both in 1723 for £6,000. He obviously needed money. It may be that the expenses of his attempts to become a Member of Parliament in the elections of 1715 and 1722 had cost too much. The lands he was mortgaging came to about 246 acres or more. He never succeeded in paying off his mortgage and he was constantly paying some of what he owed and raising other sums until, by 1740, he owed £11,000 plus unpaid interest.[4]

Henry Barker's house the Grove, together with about 110 acres of land, the trustees sold to Henry de Auverquerque, Earl of Grantham, for the outstanding sum on the mortgage of £11,000 subject to a charge for the dowry of Mary Barker, Henry's widow.[5] During his ownership of the Grove, Grantham may have made changes to the building (see below, p. 114)

The Earl of Grantham died in December 1754 and left the Grove and estate to Sir William Elliott and Frances, his wife, who were his daughter and son-in-law, for the life of them both on condition that they lived there themselves and kept it in good repair. He also left to John Hill his steward and Sarah, his wife, a newly built house with some land on the east side of the Grove for their joint lives. The estate as a whole was left to trustees, who were to sell it when the life tenants were all dead, and apply the money raised to the other purposes of the will. By July 1775 these deaths had occurred and the Grove estate was put up for sale by order of the court of chancery. Chancery was involved because some of the heirs believed that they were being kept out of their inheritance.[6]

The house and estate were advertised for sale in the *London Gazette* in December 1775 (after an abortive sale earlier in the year when not enough was offered for the estate) and one Henry Shaw bid £17,000 for the whole estate, including the house recently occupied by the Hills. On 14 December Shaw was declared the highest bidder and ordered to pay the whole of the purchase price by 27 March 1776. He had done so by 24 April and was declared to be the purchaser, and that he was making the purchase in trust for Humphrey Morice. All of this was recited in a massive deed of lease and release of 4 and 5 February 1777, involving all of those with an interest in the estate, and including Morice and his long-term friend Richard Bull, and Morice and his heirs and assigns were confirmed as the owners of the estate.[7] This purchase was subject to a mortgage which Morice had taken out with Mrs Elizabeth Joye, from whom he had borrowed £6,000. He agreed to repay this by September 1779 and Richard Bull became a trustee for the whole estate until it was repaid.[8]

4

The Estate Bought by Humphrey Morice

The estate bought by Morice was described in the deed of purchase as:

All that Capital Messuage or chief Mansion House formerly to and in possession of Henry Barker deceased and commonly called or known by the name of the Grove or by whatsoever other Name or Names the same is called or known by the name And all the outhouses Edifices and Buildings, Barns, Stables Coach houses Granaries yards Gardens Orchards Backsides whatsoever therunto belonging or appertaining or thereunto commonly used or taken part thereof And also all that park or imparked ground thereunto adjoining and belonging And all that Meadow ground lying between the said park and the River Thames containing by estimate 6 acres (be the same more or less) And also All that Ozier Ground adjoining to the said piece or parcel of Meadow Ground containing by estimate 8 acres be the same more or less

And also All that Parcel of Ground called the Pickel lying without the Court Yard Wall of the said Capital Messuage and containing by Estimation 3 Roods be the same more or less

And also All that piece or parcel of Ground Toft or Scite whereon the new erected messuage or Tenement mentioned and in and by the codicil to the Will of the said Henry late Earl of Grantham lately stood and which had been since the before stated Sale of the said Premises to the said Humphery Morice pulled down and raised by him together with the Garden to the said newly erected Messuage or Tenement lately belonging and the piece of Ground on the East Side of the said garden containing seventeen yards in length and formerly laid to and now inclosed with the said garden and which said new erected messuage or tenement garden ground and premises last mentioned were formerly in the tenure or occupation of John Hill and Sarah his wife

And all other the said meadows lands pastures and hereditaments etc formerly the estate of the said Henry Barker esquire and afterwards of the said Henry late Earl of Grantham deceased which were with the said

*capital messuage or tenement and new erected messuage or tenement
hereditaments and premises or any of them held or enjoyed or taken and
part parcel and member thereof*

*And all the right title and interest of them the said Thomas Barsham and
George Nassau Clavering Earl Cowper [Grantham's trustees] or either of
them of and to the soil of the road along the wall of the said park to
the river Thames all which premises contain by admeasurement 86 acres
and no more and were formerly supposed by the Indentures of 2 June
1723 to contain by estimation 110 acres more or less and are situate lying
and being in the said Parish of Chiswick in the said County of Middlesex
together with all ways waters trees woods imparked grounds lands
tenements hereditaments and premises hereinbefore mentioned*

*   To hold unto and to the use of the said Humphrey Morice his heirs and
assigns forever.*[1]

Thus the estate that Morice bought consisted of 86 acres, reduced from
the 110 acres mortgaged by Henry Barker. This was largely because the
Duke of Devonshire, owner of Chiswick House, had bought several
parcels of land from the trustees of the Barker estate in 1763, including
some named in the mortgage deed of 1723 and some of that included in
the 110 acres. The lands 'purchased of Mr Barker' appear separately in the
duke's rental until well on into the nineteenth century.[2]

The house that Morice bought was described in 1705–6 as a spacious,
modern building, which implies that it was built or rebuilt around 1700.
Perhaps rebuilt is the truth since T. E. Crowther, the firm who demolished
the Grove in 1928, said that they found some early pine panelling together
with some Tudor oak panelling behind the plaster panels above the dado,
although they did not say in which room. In 1897 it was said that recent
work on the house showed that the interior decorations possibly had been
by Inigo Jones, and that many of the ceilings were Italian work of 1711,
when Italian workmen were known to have been working at Chiswick
House. In addition there was in 1897 a stone let into the floor bearing the
date 1711.[3] The rate books for the period do not show any major change in
the rates paid over the period 1690 to 1720, although the rates do increase
sharply in 1749, two years after Lord Grantham bought the house. It is thus
possible that Grantham did some rebuilding and the surviving fireplace
(see below, and illustration 28) was described when sold at auction in 2012
as being possibly mid-eighteenth century. We know from illustrations that
the house had three floors until the 1830s (see below), but we do not have
a description of the interior or the grounds in 1776 when Morice bought
it. However, we do have a description of the interior drawn up by the

auction house who sold the estate in 1831, and this is borne out by a plan dated 1889, which includes an enlarged kitchen extension to be added to the east side of the house, which was never built (see illustrations 29 and 30). It is not known who commissioned these plans for altering the house but it was probably the Pullman family, who owned it at that time.[4] It seems unlikely that the main rooms of the house would have changed much between Morice's day and 1831, although Daniel Lysons says that Morice made 'considerable additions' (unspecified) to the house, and built the large stables which could accommodate thirty horses.[5]

In the sale document of 1831 the house is described as a 'freehold house adapted entirely to the Residence of a Family of Rank, without being unnecessarily large' and in a most attractive situation on the bank of the River Thames.[6] On the ground floor was 'the Grand Entrance', which we know from pictures and photographs consisted of broad stone steps with columns supporting a carved pediment on which were displayed the Barker arms, a lion rampant. Coincidentally the Morice family's arms were also a lion rampant. Through this was a hall, 'a lofty Saloon thirty feet square, a Drawing room twenty seven by twenty four feet, a Music Room, a Library twenty six by twenty four feet and a Dining Room thirty two by eighteen feet. The Floors of oak, and Plate Glass windows to the principal rooms.' In 1889 many of the walls were described as oak-panelled, with the drawing room panelled with heavy plaster mouldings, a coved ceiling and a plaster cornice. Above the cornices and centred on the panels below were richly ornamented circular panels. The staircase was oak with a carved panel stringer and a heavy moulded hand rail and carved balusters. The mantels were of Georgian carved white marble with plaster panels and carvings above.[7]

The house contained eleven upper bedrooms, presumably on the second floor, including six designed for 'visiting rooms'. The other rooms were presumably for the servants. There were six principal bed chambers (these would be on the first floor) and a billiard room. Access to this floor was by two staircases.

The rest of the house included 'everything that [could] be desired, a butler's and housekeeper's room, still and china room, servants' hall, wash-house, a laundry with two bed rooms over, a large Kitchen (an important room as will be seen from the letters since life obviously revolved around the kitchen while Morice was not at home), also a pastry room, scullery, dairy, bake and coal houses and a larder'. On the lowest story there were apparently 'an infinity of rooms adapted to various purposes, including an immensity of cool and dry cellaring'.

Outside the house was a courtyard, around which were two double-coach-houses and three stables with twenty-five stalls. These stables were perhaps those built by Morice (see above). There were five sleeping rooms over these and two hay lofts as well as other rooms. There was a farmyard with all the necessary buildings to service the 85-acre domain, which included 11 acres of osier ground on the riverbank.

The sale document says that the park has 'uniformly been the subject of invarying commendation, and for its size yields to very few in England. There is so much of Hill and Dale … the Wood and Water … that it must be Seen to be thoroughly appreciated. The Pleasure Grounds and Plantations are extensive, and laid out in accordance with the best taste.' This rather florid description is borne out by John Bowack's statement in 1705–6 that 'this seat is pleasantly situated near the Thames side: behind it are gardens, by some said to be the finest in England, and before a small park enclosed with a large brick wall'. In 1744 John Loveday of Caversham, an indefatigable tourist all around England, said that in the garden of the Grove was 'a Walk between a noble eugh [Yew] hedge in the Garden, several Eughs here also of the common shape but wich end in a Tree. Mortlack in view from the Garden Front.'[8] Daniel Lysons says that the pleasure grounds were laid out by the Earl of Grantham, which may be the case, and that the paddock contained many old walnut trees and Spanish chestnuts, 'the fruit of which has been known to produce £80 per annum.'[9] In the gardens were a pavilion and a banqueting room. One of these may be what is sometimes called the summerhouse.

The kitchen gardens were as splendid as the ornamental gardens and were enclosed by walls. These contained hot houses and succession houses (greenhouses in which plants could be brought on in succession), the whole about 150 feet long, together with a 'fruit garden' and a large conservatory. The description of the grounds in the auction document is borne out by an earlier plan of the grounds, drawn up before an abortive sale in 1826.

5

The Grove Estate from 1785 to the End

As described above, Humphrey Morice left the Grove estate and much else to Mrs Levina Luther, with the residue of his estates to her and her two half-sisters. This residue was apparently worth about £200,000. The bequests apparently occasioned a great deal of gossip.[1]

The first act carried out by Morice's executors after his will had been probated and they had received possession of the estate was to repay the mortgage which Morice had taken out with Elizabeth Joye on buying the Grove. He had not repaid it despite his agreement, and his trustees Burrell and Claxton made arrangements to repay Elizabeth Joye in February 1787. Not repaying mortgages as agreed was apparently not unusual, see below when Mrs Luther sold the Grove to the next occupant, the Revd Robert Lowth.[2]

Under Morice's will the two Bull sisters, Elizabeth and Catherine, were to receive the bulk of the estate after the death of Mrs Luther. However Catherine died in 1790 and by her will left her portion of the Morice lands to her father. Her will was apparently invalid in this part and so her sister who inherited the estates by default wanted to put into effect Catherine's intention. She therefore devised the lands to her father in January 1796.[3] By March 1805 Mrs Luther, Richard Bull and Elizabeth Bull agreed with John Claxton, by then the sole remaining trustee of Morice's will, that they would waive any right that any of them had to inherit property under Morice's will as the last one alive, and divide the residue of his estate into three parts, each of them to take one share. The Grove estate was exempted from this division, and was to be held by Mrs Luther during her lifetime, or until any animal, horse or dog as mentioned in the Morice will should remain alive. It was agreed that after this the estate would be sold and the money divided equally between the Bulls and Mrs Luther. Until then the three were to remain tenants in common. Mrs Luther agreed to give up her right to the £600 annuity left to her to look after the animals on the Grove estate since by then only one animal, a horse, was still alive.[4]

The fulfilment of this agreement was prolonged by Richard Bull dying intestate in December 1805. His daughter and sole heir was given administration of his estate in February 1806. Finally Mrs Luther agreed to purchase Elizabeth Bull's share of the Grove (which now amounted to two thirds of the whole after she had inherited the shares of her sister and father) for £16,666 13s 4d and the Grove estate was put into a trust vested in Richard Henry Alexander Bennett, brother of Levina Luther. The final document was dated 17 October 1808.[5]

Once Mrs Luther was legally sole owner of the whole estate she did not waste much time in selling the Grove estate to the Revd Robert Lowth for £29,000 on 5 July 1810. The description of the estate remained identical to that bought by Morice and still consisted of 86 acres. Lowth could not pay the whole sum for the estate so Mrs Luther agreed that £10,000 of the purchase price should be secured as a mortgage. In effect she had agreed that he should pay by instalments. Lowth agreed to pay Mrs Luther the outstanding sum in two instalments of £5,000, the first in July 1815 and the second in July 1817 at 5 per cent interest. It was agreed that Lowth could pay earlier if he wished. As will be seen he did not, in fact he died still owing £5,000 of the debt despite much raising of further mortgages on the Grove. When she died in 1814 Mrs Luther left the residue of her estate to her sister-in-law Elizabeth Bennett. £5,000 of the mortgage was still outstanding, as was the interest from July 1818, and Elizabeth Bennett had to take steps to recover the debt.[6]

Lowth died on 18 August 1822 and his will asked his trustees to sell all his property and pay his debts, putting his personal estate into trust for his family.[7] From subsequent events it is clear that there was very little personal estate left after the payment of debts, and there was not enough to pay off the mortgage on the Grove. We may gather this from an advertisement in the *Morning Post* of 11 July 1822 which advertised that a house in Chiswick, on the banks of the Thames, was available to let, furnished or unfurnished. This was 'a capital spacious Family Mansion planned for the accommodation of a very large establishment standing detached in a park of 70 acres, walled round, the mansion comprises numerous bedchambers, … stabling for twenty horses, lawns, pleasure grounds, and kitchen gardens and a pavilion commanding delightful views of the Thames. Any quantity of land may be had.' This can only be the Grove; no other estate in Chiswick fits this description. Similarly, Robert Lowth's library was advertised for sale in the *Morning Chronicle* of 13 January 1823. To make matters worse for the Lowth family two of the trustees appointed under Robert Lowth's will resigned in November 1823, leaving only one trustee, James Harrington, a clerical colleague of Lowth's.[8]

At this stage of the proceedings, in April 1824 Robert Henry Lowth, son of Robert Lowth, agreed that Levina Luther had received £5,000 of the sum owing plus interest due, and that his father's personal estate had proved insufficient to discharge the remaining £5,000. The Lowths had therefore asked one William Ford to lend them the remaining £5,000 at interest, which he had done, and the original mortgage was paid off. Robert Henry Lowth agreed to repay this second mortgage by 6 March 1831 and Ford agreed to assign the estate to a designated person on that date.[9]

In 1826 the Lowths apparently made another attempt to raise money from the estate by auctioning eleven acres of osier ground, part of the estate. This was advertised in four lots as very productive and worth £300 per year. Osiers were valuable for making baskets for market produce, Chiswick and the neighbouring Brentford were full of market gardens. Lot 1 was specifically mentioned as being close to Brentford. Interestingly, in the plan which accompanied the auction document the garden of the house is shown divided into 'convenient lots for the erection of villas'. This land was also advertised as containing several acres of valuable brick earth, as was often the case in this area. The house itself with its kitchen gardens, pleasure grounds, walks and park was advertised as available if desired, albeit possibly by then in the middle of the 'desirable villas'.[10] There is no record that the sale took place and the osier ground was still part of the estate in 1831 when the whole estate was sold. The area around the house was not developed until the end of the nineteenth century.

In pursuance of the agreement to pay the mortgage in 1831, the Grove estate was put up for auction. It was first advertised for sale on 11 June as the handsome stone edifice called 'Grove Mansion and Demesne' and advertisements appeared over the next four weeks, with the auction being set for 14 July.[11] The estate was described as having 11 acres of osier grounds on the banks of the river, together with extensive walled gardens encompassed by lofty walls and ornamented by a range of hot and succession houses 150 feet long, and in the French garden was a conservatory 'of great extent'. The park was of 85 acres with much full-grown timber. Interestingly in the advertisements the house was not mentioned, but it was described in the auction document. The whole estate was bought by the Duke of Devonshire for £15,750. There exists a copy of the auction document with a memorandum dated 23 July 1831 and signed by Benjamin Currey, the Duke's agent and solicitor, stating the sale price and underneath that is an agreement by James Harrington, sole remaining trustee of Robert Lowth, to sell the property. It seems likely that Harrington was very pleased to sign this. The duke paid £17,175 in total for the estate, which included £1,425 for the timber.[12]

That the Lowths had very little money even before Robert Lowth senior died is shown by the fact that they did not pay the rent due on Warren Wall field (a field just south of the boundary of the Grove estate) that they were renting from the Duke of Devonshire. The Duke's rentals record payment of the rent for the field from 1811 to 1818 but by 1819 Lowth was in arrears with his payments, and he did not pay at all in 1820, and by 1825 Mrs Lowth was even more in arrears. By 1827 Mr Joseph Jessop was paying rent for fruit trees in Warren Wall field 'late in the occupation of Mrs Lowth'. The Duke had obviously grown tired of waiting for his rent. Mrs Lowth was not paying the church rates either from 1826 until she left in 1830. The house was empty in 1831.[13] Interestingly, given the apparent state of the Lowth finances the auction particulars for the estate note that the mansion 'stands in need of ornamental reparation', perhaps auctioneers' language for 'needs total redecoration'.

There is nothing in the Duke of Devonshire's rentals for the Grove in 1831 and 1832, although different men were paid to look after the house and grounds, and 2 acres and thirty-eight roods of potatoes were planted in the grounds. By January 1833 George Spencer Ridgeway was paying £130 rent to the Duke to live in Grove House. Ridgeway was the Duke's receiver in Chiswick, and it is interesting to speculate that he may have been installed in the house to oversee the alterations made by the Duke, who seems to have removed the entire top floor of the house at this time. This work may have been carried out by Decimus Burton, the architect, who was working for the Duke in 1835 in Chiswick.[14]

Ridgeway stayed at the Grove until midsummer 1836 when he was replaced as tenant by Septimus Burton, an older brother of Decimus. It is tempting to wonder if it was Decimus who told Septimus about the Grove. Septimus rented the Grove and only 13 acres of land; the rest was probably being farmed by Joseph Jessop, who rented a great deal of the Duke's land. Septimus also paid £7 interest every year for the outlay by the Duke on an iron fence and for a grapery. Burton remained at the Grove until 1842 when he died, aged only 48. He was buried in Chiswick parish church with his wife and baby son, who had both died two years earlier.[15]

Following Septimus Burton were a series of tenants; Richard Gurney from 1844 to 1853, succeeded by Joseph Gurney by 1855. After him Dr Cowan lived there from 1856 until 1861. A Mr Robert Prowett started his tenancy in the summer of 1861, left in 1870 and was followed by a John Pullman. By 1872 the Duke had sold the Grove and the new owners were the Pullman family. The house was occupied by Colonel Robert Mulliner, but by 1882 the Pullmans had moved back and remained there until 1886.

From 1888 to 1894 Joseph Atkins Borsley was living in the Grove, which was still owned by the Pullmans.[16]

In 1895 the Grove was occupied by Lt Colonel Robert Shipway, who rented it from Mr Pullman until 1898, when he bought the house. Shipway was a Middlesex county councillor and a JP. He was active in the Volunteers, hence his military rank. The family were breeches makers in Oxford Street, from which he obtained his wealth, and his chief claim to fame is that he bought Hogarth House, once the country residence of William Hogarth, rescuing it from the threat of demolition, and presented it to Middlesex County Council to be opened to the public. He made no more than minor alterations to the Grove and he was the last owner, living there until 1928 when he died. After this the house was demolished to make way for the 'villas' first mentioned in 1826.[17]

There is a local legend that the house was not destroyed but taken down carefully and transferred to America, where it was rebuilt. This has never been confirmed, and the fact that one of the fireplaces is known to have been sold to the Huntington Library and Art Collection in California would seem to show that at least some parts of the house were sold as architectural salvage. The fireplace remained on display at the Huntington Art Gallery until recently as part of the Quinn Room, a composite of architectural elements from several different historic English houses. Only the one fireplace was from the Grove. This room was recently sold at auction and it is not known where it is now. The Metropolitan Museum of Art in New York also owns two items said to have come from the Grove: two fragments of baluster, one wood and one metal.[18]

Appendix 1: Morice's Associates & Friends

Bennett: Richard Henry Alexander Bennett was the son of Bennett Alexander Bennett by his wife Mary, daughter of Benjamin Ash, and later wife of Richard Bull (see below). They had two children, Richard (born about 1742) and Levina (see below). Bennett was introduced to Morice by his stepfather Richard Bull, and sat for Newport, Cornwall, a seat in Morice's patronage, from 1770–4 when he was a moderately active Member of Parliament. In 1766 he married Elizabeth Amelia, sister of Peter Burrell (see below). As well as being linked by marriage, the group including the Bulls and the Bennetts, together with Richard Bennett's brother in law Peter Burrell and John Claxton, a relative of Morice, as well as Morice himself, acted together in legal matters. An example of this is a deed in the Essex Record Office (dated after 1750) to which the parties include R. H. A. Bennett; R. H. A. Bennett's wife Elizabeth Amelia; Peter Burrell, the father of Elizabeth Amelia Bennett; William Burrell, brother of Peter and one of Morice's executors; and Morice himself. Similarly, a deed in the Cornwall Record Office of 1805 associates Levina Luther; Richard Bull, her stepfather; Elizabeth Bull, her half-sister; and John Claxton, one of Morice's executors.[1] The Bennetts, the Bulls and John Luther all came originally from the Ongar district of Essex. Towards the end of his life, R. H. A. Bennett bought the estate in the Isle of Wight to which Richard Bull had moved earlier. He died in 1814.

Bull: Richard Bull was a close associate of Morice for many years, politically, in business matters and socially. He was of Ongar and of North Court Shorwell, Isle of Wight, and in a sense the centre of the group around Morice, who apparently visited often. In 1747 Bull married Mary, daughter of Benjamin Ash, also of Ongar, and the widow of B. A. Bennett. Mary already had two children from her first marriage, Richard Henry Alexander Bennett and Levina, wife of John Luther. Richard Bull and Mary had two daughters together, Elizabeth and Catherine Susanna. Bull and Morice probably first met at Cambridge. Bull was at Trinity Hall from 1743 to 1744, and while Morice was there in 1740–41, his name was not removed from the books until 1744 so he may well have been there at intervals over the period of Bull's residence. They were close colleagues from then until Morice's death, as seen above. This was both social as well as for business; for example, Morice was a frequent guest at North Court, Bull's house in the Isle of Wight.[2] Additionally Bull sat as MP for Newport, Cornwall, a seat in the patronage of Morice, from 1756 until 1780, when Morice sold his boroughs. Bull then left Parliament. His chief claim to fame is that he was a collector of engravings, particularly portraits, which he inserted into books to illustrate them, the practice of extra illustration or Grangerising, named after the man to whom the practice was first attributed. The practice became a craze, and Walpole blamed Bull for causing the price of engravings to rise from a few shillings to several pounds each. Bull was left an annuity of £500 in Morice's will, and his daughters were left £100 to 'share and share alike', as well as being his residuary legatees after Levina Luther (see below).[3] Bull died in 1805.

Burrell: Peter Burrell was MP for Morice's seat of Launceston 1759–68 and MP for Totnes (not one of Morice's seats) 1768–74. His daughter Elizabeth Amelia married R. H. A. Bennett. He died in 1775.

Burrell: Sir William Burrell was one of Morice's executors. Brother of Peter Burrell and MP for their family seat of Haslemere 1768–74. He was a lawyer, a member of Doctors' Commons – the court for ecclesiastical and admiralty cases – for a large part of his career, and a commissioner of excise. He was a respected advocate. He was a fellow of the Society of Antiquaries and compiler of what would have been (if he could have brought it to publication) an excellent history of the county of Sussex. He was left £1,000 by Morice for his 'trouble' in administering Morice's will. He died in 1796.[4]

Claxton: John Claxton was one of Morice's executors together with William Burrell. Claxton was not a politician like most of Morice's close associates but a lawyer, perhaps a barrister of Lincoln's Inn, also a fellow of the Society of Antiquaries. He was related to Morice since Morice's father had married firstly Judith Sandes, a younger daughter of Thomas Sandes, a London merchant, and John Claxton, grandfather of the executor, had married Sarah Sandes, Judith's sister. Morice, as the son of his father's second marriage was thus a distant cousin of John Claxton. As well as being related to him, presumably Morice used Claxton for his legal expertise. After the death of Morice, who had left him £1,000 for his trouble as executor, Claxton remained associated with Mrs Luther and Richard Bull, for example acting with them two years before he died as a witness in a property transaction to an estate in Cornwall, the property of Mrs Luther. He died in 1811.

Lee: Sir George Lee was the fourth son of Sir Thomas Lee, 2nd Baronet. He married Judith, daughter of Humphrey Morice senior by his first wife Judith Sandes. Judith was one of Humphrey Morice junior's older half-sisters. Sir George Lee was MP for Launceston, one of Morice's parliamentary seats in 1754–8. He died in 1758.

Lee: Sir William Lee, 4th Baronet was the son of Sir Thomas Lee, 3rd Baronet and his wife Elizabeth Sandes (sister of Judith Sandes who married Humphrey Morice senior), and thus the nephew of Sir George and cousin to Humphrey Morice junior and his older half-sisters.

Luther: Mrs Levina Luther inherited the Grove and the estate from Morice as described. There has been much speculation about Mrs Luther and why Morice should have left her such a magnificent legacy. It has always been assumed that she must have been a relative of his, perhaps with a connection through her mother Mary Ash. This would appear to be unlikely since Benjamin Ash, Mary's father, describes himself as a 'yeoman' in his will of 1725/6[5] and seems to have had no powerful connections. Lewis Namier cites a letter of Charles Phillips, MP for Camelford, to Lord Newcastle in 1756 concerning Richard Bull (see above) and referring to him as Morice's 'relative' but this was almost certainly speculation based on his close political relations with Bull.[6] Any relationship between Mrs Luther and Morice must have been very distant indeed and his connection with her seems to have been through a group of friends and colleagues, that is Richard Bull and the Bennett family, with whom Morice had been associated in Parliament and socially.

Levina Luther was born Levina Bennett in about 1744, the younger child of Mary Ash and Bennett Alexander Bennett. Her unusual name was that of her grandmother, daughter of Sir Levinus Bennett. Her father died in 1745 and her mother married Richard Bull in 1747. A picture of the young Levina was painted in about 1747 as part of a group including her mother, brother and Richard Bull, perhaps to commemorate the marriage (see illustration 2). We know nothing of her life from then until 1762, when she married John Luther of Myles, near Ongar where the Bulls lived. It does not seem as if Luther was one of the Bull/Bennett group around Morice, and it appears that Morice did not have a very high opinion of him since he specified in his will that Mrs Luther was to have full control of all that she was left despite her 'coverture', the legal principle that a married woman was under the protection and authority of her husband. The Luthers had two children, both of whom died in their father's lifetime, but it seems that the marriage was not a particularly happy one because two years after the wedding Luther fled to France in (apparently) a separation from his wife, and although persuaded by his friend Richard Watson to return, he still remained separated from his wife, who lived with her mother and step-father.[7] Luther was an MP for the Essex seat for twenty years but there is no record of his having spoken in the House in that time. He was apparently a rather ineffectual man. He died in 1786, a few months after Morice. His will confirms the marriage settlement on his wife and grants her £750 per annum out of his estate in pursuance of the settlement.[8] This was the only reference to her in the will. His estates he left to his nephew and to his friend Richard Watson.

Whatever the character of her husband Mrs Luther was obviously not ineffectual. She was apparently popular in her social circle and enjoyed singing. The Bull/Bennett circle obviously enjoyed singing and listening to music, frequently attending the opera. Catherine Bull, one of Richard Bull's daughters, lent an opera ticket to Fanny D'Arblay from which it appears that she had some kind of season ticket, and the great castrato Guiseppe Millico wrote to Elizabeth Bull, Richard Bull's other daughter, in friendly terms. Pinkerton, in his article on Richard Bull, says that Mrs Luther was known to her step-family as the 'Cara'. This may be so, although Richard Bull, in a letter to (probably) a Miss Carter in 1804, says that he hopes 'the dear Cara' was well and that her children were well. Mrs Luther had no living children.[9]

After Mrs Luther inherited the Grove we do not know how much time she spent there. She is named as of Charles Street, Berkeley Square in a deed of 1794 but this may merely be a London address which she used sometimes.[10] We have no references to her meeting her neighbours in Chiswick. For later events after she inherited the estate see **The Grove Estate from 1785 to the End,** pp. 117-19

Morice: Anne Morice was the half-sister and only remaining close relative of Morice when she died. We know little about her; the only letters surviving are a group of eight letters, now in the Buckinghamshire Record Office, which are purely social ones to her cousin Sir William Lee.[11] We learn little more about her from the Grove letters. There are scattered references to old servants of hers, and we can gather that she was also fond of animals since Elizabeth Phillips, an old servant of hers, was looking after dogs that had belonged to Anne Morice.[12] Anne Morice died in 1777 and was buried on 6 November in the church of St Peter le Poer in Broad Street in London, where her parents were also buried.

Appendix 2: The Morice Portraits

There are two portraits of Morice in existence. There is a reclining full-length portrait and also a copy of it, and there are several head-and-shoulder portraits, which were painted at about the same time as the reclining full-length version for presentation to friends and relations.

These portraits are by Pompeo Batoni. The original full-length one was painted in 1762 in the artist's studio in Rome. Batoni was an artist who was much admired by British gentry on the Grand Tour in the eighteenth century, and many of them were eager to have him paint their portrait when they reached Rome. This Morice portrait is now owned by Sir James and Lady Graham, Norton Conyers, North Yorkshire. As seen in illustration 3, Morice is dressed in a suit of blue-shot silk (which certainly would not have been worn for hunting) and is posed with his whippets, perhaps his own hunting dogs, and with the game shot that day in front of him, an interesting setting for an animal lover. It has been suggested that the reclining posture was adopted to conceal Morice's short stature. This pose is unique in Batoni's work, and unusual in the work of other contemporary artists. The background to the portrait has been identified as the Torre Leonina and the Torre dei Venti as seen from outside the walls of the Vatican gardens, an unusual setting for Batoni and we may wonder if the unusual pose and the use of this background was suggested by Morice. It is possible that Morice was inspired to choose the pose by another Batoni painting, of Diana and Cupid, which he must have seen in the painter's studio and bought from there in 1762. With a mixture of a reclining figure, dogs and a landscape in the background it is reminiscent of the pose of the Morice portrait, and the two may have been hung together.[1]

It seems certain that the portrait in illustration 3 is the original, painted for Morice. In this case it would have been the one hung at the Grove and inherited by Mrs Luther, but there is no mention of the Morice family pictures in Mrs Luther's will. Mrs Luther made her sister-in-law,

Elizabeth Amelia Bennett, her residuary legatee, and this presumably included the family portraits, but after that the descent is unknown. The portrait was owned from sometime after 1850 by Fulke Greville-Nugent, later first Lord Greville, and descended from him to the Graham family. Why Greville should have it is not known. Greville's wife was a Cecil and included Bennett amongst her many Christian names, but no family connection between her and Elizabeth Amelia Bennett seems to exist.[2]

At least one other copy of this full-length portrait exists. It was until recently owned by the late Sir Brinsley Ford. This picture seems certain to be the copy that Morice had made for his cousin Sir William Lee, and which hung in the Lee mansion of Hartwell until the house was sold in 1938. Morice had apparently been asked by Sir William for a copy of his portrait, perhaps soon after it was painted, and Morice had agreed to have one made but had not fulfilled his promise by 1768. In that year he offered to give the original picture to Sir William who apparently refused to accept it, and two years later Morice had a copy made in Rome, probably in Batoni's studio, from what he says in a letter to Sir William. Thus it seems that the original was still in Rome eight years after it was painted. This copy was sent to Sir William in 1770.[3]

As well as the full-length portrait there is a half-length, which exists in several versions. These were painted by Batoni at the same time as the full-length picture for Morice to give to friends and relations. These smaller portraits were frequently commissioned by sitters. The one shown in illustration 1 is now owned by the Wadsworth Atheneum Museum of Art, Hartford, Connecticut, and was probably once owned by the 1st Duke of Sutherland. The Duke was a contemporary of Morice, but we know of no connection between them. Other copies exist; one of them, sold in 1993 at Sotheby's, was said to have descended in the Molesworth family.[4] This is quite possible since Sir John Molesworth, the 4th Baronet, married Barbara, younger sister of Sir William Morice, the last Morice baronet, and Morice might have given a copy to the family.

Appendix 3: The Animals & Their Health & Treatment

There are very many references to animals in the letters. It seems in many ways as if passing on news of the state of health of the dogs and horses was a major reason for writing the letters. Thus it seemed important to explain what exactly the animals were suffering from, since the various ailments, and the anatomy of horses, are not as familiar to most people now as they would have been in the past. We were fortunate to be able to ask a friend, the late Philip Daykin, an experienced vet, a lecturer at the Royal Veterinary College and research director of a large pharmaceutical company, to comment on the ailments of the animals and their treatment. All comments on these matters are derived from him and are printed as notes to the letters. In general Philip recorded that he felt that Bishop was obviously very experienced and knowledgeable in the ways of animals and their care, and that he probably treated them as well as he was able, according to the best practice known at his time.

Appendix 4: Will of Humphrey Morice

Transcribed from the will register at the National Archives by Mary King, reference PROB 11/1139, with occasional readings checked from the original copy at PROB 10/3005.

Some spelling has been modernised, and paragraphs and minimal punctuation have been added to make the text easier to read. The modern spelling of some place names has been added in square brackets after the version in the will.

The Right Honourable Humphrey Morice Esquire, late one of his Majesty's most Honourable Privy Council

This is the last Will and Testament of me the Right Honourable Humphrey Morice of the Grove in the Parish of Chiswick in the County of Middlesex Esquire one of his Majesty's most Honourable Privy Council made in manner following that is to say I desire that my Body may be interred in a private manner in the Vault in the Burying Ground of Wandsworth Hill in the County of Surrey wherein my Mother and other Relations are Buryed.

And I desire that all my Servants both Male and Female may continue in my House three calendar Months after my decease and that my Executors hereinafter named will pay to each of them half a Guinea a week during that time for board wages besides Coals Candles and such other Articles as are usually allowed to Servants when at Board Wages.

And I give all my wearing Apparel whatsoever unto my Servant Richard Deale together with my repeating Watch No. 17,527. But as to my three other repeating Watches and all my Diamond Rings and Buckles I give and desire the same to be disposed of unto such Persons and in such manner as I shall mention in a Writing or Letter that I shall leave with this my Will.

And I give and bequeath the Annuity or Yearly Sum of five hundred pounds which I purchased of William Gray Esquire and which is charged or secured upon his Estate in the Island of Jamaica during the joint lives of Richard Bull of Stratton Street Piccadilly in the County of Middlesex Esquire and my own life and for the life of the survivor. And all the arrears thereof and all my Right and Interest therein and thereto during the life of the said Richard Bull, unto him the said Richard Bull to and for his own Use and Benefit.

And I give and bequeath the Annuity or Yearly Sum of one hundred pounds which I am also entitled to during the joint lives of the two Daughters of the said Richard Bull and the life of the survivor of them which I also purchased of the said William Gray and which is also Charged or Secured upon his Estate in the said Island of Jamaica. And all Arrears thereof and all my Right and Interest therein, unto the said two Daughters of the said Richard Bull equally share and share alike during their joint lives and to the survivor of them during his life to and for their and her own Use and Benefit.

And I give and bequeath the Annuity or Yearly Sum of three hundred pounds which I purchased of Thomas Davison Esquire and which is charged upon his Estate called Preston Plantation in the said Island of Jamaica for and during the lives of myself and of Ann, Jane and Albinia Reeve Spinsters, Daughters of Dame Jane Reeve of Holyport in the County of Berks and for the lives and life of the survivors and survivor of them. And all Arrears thereof and all my Right and Interest of and in the said last mentioned Annuity unto her the said Dame Jane Reeve her Heirs and Assigns to and for her and their own use and benefit.

And I give and devise all my Freehold Messuages Lands Tenements Hereditaments and Real Estate whatsoever situate lying and being at Chipstead and Meestham [Merstham] in the said County of Surrey with their and every of their Rights Members and Appurtenances unto John Claxton of Shirley in the County of Surrey Esquire his Heirs and Assigns To the only proper use and behoof of the said John Claxton his Heirs and Assigns for ever.

And I give and bequeath all that my Messuage Tenement or Dwelling house situate in Dover Street in the said County of Middlesex with the Stables Buildings and Appurtenances thereunto belonging. And also all that my Manor or Lordship of Wood Walton in the County of Huntingdon. And all my Messuages Farms Lands Tenements and Hereditaments to the said Manor or Lordship belonging or in anywise appertaining And all my Estate Right Title and Interest in and to the same respectively with their and every of their Rights Members and Appurtenances unto William Burrell of Harley Street Cavendish Square in the County of Middlesex Esquire and the said John Claxton their Heirs and Assigns To the use and behoof of them the said William Burrell and John Claxton their Heirs and Assigns absolutely. But nevertheless upon the Trusts and to and for the several Intents and Purposes hereinafter expressed and declared of and concerning the same (that is to say) upon Trust that they the said William Burrell and John Claxton or the survivor of them or the Heirs or Assigns of such survivor shall and do with all convenient speed after my decease sell dispose of and absolutely convey the said Messuage or Tenement and premises in Dover Street and all and singular the Manor Messuages Farms Hereditaments and other premises so devised to them unto such person or persons as shall be willing to purchase the same for the best price that can be reasonably got for same. And such purchaser or purchasers upon payment of his her or their purchase Money unto and obtaining a Receipt or Receipts for the same from my said Trustees or the survivor of them or the Heirs or Assigns of such survivor shall not afterwards be liable to see to the application thereof nor be answerable for the Loss Misapplication or Nonapplication of the same and upon Trust that they the said William Burrell and John Claxton and the survivor of them and the Executors or Administrators of such survivor shall and do stand possessed of the Money to arise by such sale or sales and dispose of the same in such manner to such person and persons as is and are hereinafter mentioned and expressed concerning the same.

And I give and bequeath the capital sum of twelve thousand four hundred and fifty two pounds Bank Stock now standing in my name and the Capital Sum of three thousand seven hundred and fifty pounds East India Stock also standing in my name and all such other Bank Stock and East India Stock as I may be possessed of or entitled to at the time of my decease unto the said William Burrell and John Claxton their Executors Administrators and Assigns upon the several Trusts and to and for the several Intents and Purposes hereinafter mentioned and declared of and concerning the same.

And with regard to all my plate and pictures in my Houses both in Dover Street and at the Grove or elsewhere and all my Household Goods and Furniture and all the Rest and Residue of my personal Estate consisting of Three Per Centum Consolidated Bank Annuities, East India Annuities, Three per Cent Annuities, Million Bank Stock, South Sea Annuities Exchequer Annuities, Moneys and Securitys for Money and all other Effects whatsoever and wheresoever (except the Beds Household Goods and Furniture in and about my said Mansion House called the Grove and except portraits of relations and other friends but not the plate and other pictures and except all my live and dead stock in and about the same and the Lands there in my own occupation which

Furniture Portraits Live and Dead Stock I shall dispose of in manner hereinafter mentioned) unto the said William Burrell and John Claxton their Executors Administrators and Assigns upon Trust that they the said William Burrell and John Claxton and the survivor of them and the Executors Administrators and Assigns of such survivor shall and do as soon as conveniently may be after my decease sell and absolutely dispose of the said plate pictures and Household Furniture (except as aforesaid) for the most Money that can be reasonably had or gotten for the same and shall and do sell and convert into Money all such other part and parts of the residue of my personal Estate as shall not consist of Money upon Trust that they the said William Burrell and John Claxton and the survivor of them and the Executors Administrators and Assigns of such survivor shall and do stand possessed of and interested in the Money to arise or be produced by such Sale or Sales.

And all such and so much of the Residue of my personal Estate as shall consist of Money together with all the Money to arise by the Sale or Sales of my said Messuage or Tenement and premises in Dover Street aforesaid and the said Manor Hereditaments and Premises in the said County of Huntingdon hereby directed to be sold as hereinbefore is mentioned upon the Trusts and to and for the Intents and Purposes hereinafter mentioned concerning the same (that is to say) In the first place by and out of such Money to pay and satisfy all my just Debts and Funeral Expenses and in the next place thereout to pay the Sum of One hundred pounds to the Governors of the Lying in Hospital for Unmarried Women situate near Oxford Road in the County of Middlesex. The like sum of one hundred pounds to the Governors of the Small Pox Hospital Cold Bath Fields and the like sum of one hundred pounds to the Governors of the Foundling Hospital in the said County of Middlesex the said three several Legacies to be applied in such manner as the said Governors shall think fit for the benefit of the said Charitable Establishments.

And to pay to the poor of the Parish of Wandsworth aforesaid the sum of one hundred pounds and to the poor of the parish of Chiswick aforesaid the like sum of one hundred pounds and to the poor of the parish of Wood Walton aforesaid the further sum of one hundred pounds the same to be respectively paid to and divided amongst such poor people of the said several parishes and in such shares and proportion as my said Trustees shall think fit.

And also to pay the sum of one hundred pounds to Charlotte Allan of the City of Bath spinster, and the sum of Five hundred pounds unto John Allan Junior now apprentice to Messieurs Lane and Bicknell of Cheapside London Linnen Drapers, And the further sum of one hundred pounds unto Hannah Allan the sister of the said Charlotte and John Allan.

And then to pay or retain to themselves my said Trustees the sum of one Thousand pounds each for their trouble in the Execution of this my Will.

And likewise to pay all such other Legacies or Sums of Money as I may by any Codicil or Codicils to this my Will give direct or appoint all which said several Legacies (except the Legacy to the said John Allan) I order and direct to be paid within twelve months from the time of my decease and the said Legacy to the said John Allan I order to be paid to him as soon as his apprenticeship shall be expired.

And from and after the several payments herein before mentioned then upon Trust that the said William Burrell and John Claxton and the survivor of them and the Executors and Administrators of such survivor shall and do with all convenient speed place out and invest all the residue of the Money which shall remain after the payments aforesaid in their own names or in the name of the survivor of them his Executors or Administrators at Interest upon such Government or real securities or other Security or Securitys either public or private as they or the survivor of them his Executors or Administrators shall from time to time think fit and approve of. And also change the Securities for the same from time to time during the continuance of the said Trusts hereinafter declared when and so often as they shall think it proper and expedient so to do.

And upon Trust that they the said William Burrell and John Claxton and the survivor of them and the Executors Administrators and Assigns of such survivor shall and do pay apply and dispose of the Interest and Dividends which shall from time to time accrue thereon or arise therefrom during the natural life of Mrs Levina Luther the wife of John Luther of Myles's in the County of Essex Esquire unto such person or persons and for such intents and purposes as the said Levina Luther shall from time to time notwithstanding her Coverture by Note or Writing under her hand direct or appoint and in default of such direction or appointment shall and do pay the same into the proper hands of her the said Levina Luther from time to during her life for her own sole and separate use and Benefit notwithstanding her present or any future Coverture and I order and direct that the same shall not be subject or liable to the power Control Debts Forfeitures or Engagements of her present or any after taken Husband and that the Receipt or Receipts of the said Levina Luther or of such person or persons to whom she shall from time to time so direct the same to be paid as aforesaid shall from time to time notwithstanding her present or future Coverture be a good and sufficient Discharge and Discharges for so much of such Interest or Dividends as in such Receipt or Receipts shall be expressed to be received and from and after the decease of the said Levina Luther Then upon Trust that they the said William Burrell and John Claxton or the survivor of them or the Executors or Administrators of such survivor shall and do pay and dispose of all such Trust Monies or transfer the Security or Security's wherein the same shall be invested unto Elizabeth Bull and Catherine Bull Spinsters Daughters of Richard Bull of Stratton Street London Esquire their respective Executors Administrators and Assigns to be equally divided between them share and share alike to and for their own proper use and Benefit.

And with regard to the family portraits Beds Household Goods and Furniture live and dead stock in and about my said Mansion House called the Grove and the Lands there in my own occupation I give and bequeath the same unto the said Levina Luther absolutely for her own use exclusive of and independent of her said Husband. And I give and devise all that my said Capital Mansion House called the Grove and all my Lands Tenements and Hereditaments whatsoever and of what nature or kind soever situate lying and being at the Grove and in the parish of Chiswick in the said County of Middlesex with their and every of their appurtenances unto the said William Burrell and John Claxton and their Heirs To the several uses Intents and Purposes upon the Trusts and under and subject to the Powers Provisoes Limitations and Declarations hereinafter expressed and declared of and concerning the same that is to say to the use of them the said William Burrell and John Claxton their Heirs and Assigns during the term of the natural life of the said Levina Luther the Wife of the said John Luther. But nevertheless upon the Trusts and to and for the Intents and Purposes hereinafter mentioned and declared and from and after the decease of the said Levina Luther Then to the use and behoof of the said Elizabeth Bull and Catherine Bull their Heirs and Assigns for ever share and share alike and they to take as Tenants in common and not as joint Tenants and I do hereby declare my Will to be that the said Capital Mansion House Lands Tenements and Hereditaments so limited to the said William Burrell and John Claxton their Heirs and Assigns during the natural life of the said Levina Luther as aforesaid are respectively so limitted to them upon Trust that they the said William Burrell and John Claxton and the survivor of them and the Heirs and Assigns of such survivor shall and do from time to time during the life of the said Levina Luther permit and suffer her the said Levina Luther to hold use occupy and enjoy the same without being subject or liable to the power control Debts Forfeiture or Engagements of her present or any after taken Husband. But my Mind and Will is that the same shall not be demised or let out on Lease to any Person or Persons whatsoever.

And I give and devise all those my several Manors of Cliston otherwise Broad Clist [Broad Clyst], Bradworthy, Sutcombe, Norcott [Northcott], Luffincott, Whyddon, Stoddiscombe, Halwell, and South Milton in the County of Devon, and also all those my Manors of Trethew and Little Petherick in the County of Cornwall, and all my Messuages Farms Lands Tenements and Hereditaments to the said several Manors and every or any of them belonging or in any wise appertaining, and also all other my Manors Messuages Tenements and Hereditaments in the said Counties of Devon and Cornwall or elsewhere in the Kingdom of Great Britain (not by me otherwise disposed of) with their and every of their Rights Members aed appurtenances unto the said William Burrell and John Claxton their Heirs and Assigns To the several uses Intents and Purposes and upon the Trusts and under and subject to the Powers Declarations and Limitations hereinafter expressed and declared of and concerning the same respectively (that is to say) To the use Intent and Purpose that they the said William Burrell and John Claxton and the survivor of them or the Heirs Executors or Administrators of such survivor shall and do in the first place by and out of the Rents Issues and Profits of the said several Manors Hereditaments and Premises deduct and set apart annually the Sum of Six Hundred Pounds and pay apply and dispose of the same unto such person or persons in such manner and for such purposes as I shall mention in a Writing or Letter that I shall leave with this my Will at the time of my decease.

And to the use Intent and Purpose that my Servant John Allan or his Assigns shall and may yearly and every year for and during the term of his natural life have receive and take one Annuity or Yearly Rent Charge of one hundred Pounds of lawful Money of Great Britain to be yearly issuing and going out of all and singular the said last mentioned Manors Messuages Lands Tenements and Hereditaments.

And to the use Intent and purpose that my Servant Thomas Stracey or his Assigns shall and may yearly and every year for and during the term of his natural life have receive and take one Annuity or Yearly Rent Charge of sixty Pounds of like lawful Money of Great Britain.

And to the use Intent and Purpose that my said Servant Richard Deale or his Assigns shall and may yearly and every year for and during the term of his natural life have receive and take one Annuity or Yearly Rent Charge of one hundred and fifty Pounds of like lawful Money.

And to the further use Intent and purpose that my Servant Richard Harris or his Assigns shall and may yearly and every year for and during the term of his natural life have receive and take one Annuity or Yearly Rent Charge of Forty Pounds of like lawful Money.

And to this further use Intent and purpose that Richard Harris Son of the said Richard Harris or his Assigns shall and may yearly and every year for and during the term of his natural life have receive and take one Annuity or yearly Rent Charge of Ten Pounds of like lawful Money.

And to this further use Intent and purpose that my Servant Jane Power or her Assigns shall and may yearly and every year for and during the term of her natural life have receive and take one Annuity or Yearly Rent Charge of Thirty Pounds of like Money.

And to the further use Intent and purpose that my Servant Susannah Starke or her Assigns shall and may yearly and every year for and during the term of her natural life have receive and take one Annuity or Yearly Rent Charge of Thirty Pounds of like Money.

And to the use Intent and purpose that my Servant Elizabeth Roberts or her Assigns shall and may yearly and every year for and during the term of her natural life have receive and take one Annuity or Yearly Rent Charge of Thirty Pounds of like Money.

And to the further use Intent and purpose that Elizabeth Wingood of Kensington Square in the said County of Middlesex Widow or her Assigns shall and may yearly and every year for and during the term of her natural life have receive and take one Annuity or Yearly Rent Charge of Fifty Pounds of like Money.

And to the further use Intent and purpose that my Godson Henry Kent Son of Joseph Kent of Colton in Staffordshire or his Assigns shall and may yearly and every year for and during the term of his natural life have receive and take one other Annuity or Yearly Rent Charge of Fifty Pounds of like Money.

And to the further use Intent and purpose that the said John Allan the Younger or his Assigns shall and may yearly and every year for and during the term of his natural life have receive and take one Annuity or Yearly Rent Charge of Forty Pounds of like Money.

And to the further use Intent and Purpose that James Greenfield now an apprentice to Mr Hearne a Collarmaker at Hammersmith in the said County of Middlesex and his Assigns shall and may yearly and every year during the term of his natural life have receive and take one Annuity or Yearly Rent Charge of Twenty pounds of like Money.

And to the use Intent and purpose that such other Annuities or Yearly Rent Charges may be paid as I shall or may by any Codicil or Codicils to this my Will Give Direct or Appoint.

All which said several Annuities or Yearly Rent Charges of One hundred pounds to the said John Allan, Sixty pounds to the said Thomas Stracey, One hundred and fifty pounds to the said Richard Deale, Forty pounds to the said Richard Harris the Father, Ten pounds to the said Richard Harris the Son, Thirty pounds to the said Jane Power, Thirty pounds to the said Susan Starke, Thirty pounds to the said Elizabeth Roberts, Fifty pounds to the said Elizabeth Wingood, Fifty pounds to the said Henry Kent, Forty pounds to the said John Allan the Younger and Twenty pounds to the said James Greenfield and such other Annuities or Yearly Rent Charges as aforesaid are to be likewise yearly issuing and going out of all and singular the said last mentioned Manors Messuages Lands Tenements and Hereditaments and all the said several annuities are to be respectively paid and payable free from all Taxes and Deductions to them the said John Allan, Thomas Stracey, Richard Deale, Richard Harris the Father, Richard Harris the Son, Jane Power, Susan Starke, Elizabeth Roberts, Elizabeth Wingood, Henry Kent, John Allan the Younger and James Greenfield and such other annuitant or annuitants as aforesaid or their respective assigns half yearly (that is to say) at Michaelmas Day and Lady Day in every year by equal half yearly payments And the first payment of such annuities respectively to begin and be made on such of the said Feasts or Days of Payment as shall first happen next after my decease.

And to and for this further use Intent and Purpose that in case the said above mentioned several annual sums or Yearly Rent Charges or any of them or any part or parts of the said several annuities shall at any time or times be behind or unpaid by the space of Thirty Days next after either of the said Feasts or Days of Payment whereon the same ought to be paid as aforesaid then and from thenceforth and so often it shall and may be lawful to and for the said several annuitants respectively and their several and respective Assigns during the respective lives of such annuitants into and upon the said Manors Messuages Lands Tenements and Premises hereby charged with the payment thereof and into and upon every or any part or parts thereof to enter and distrain and the distress and distresses then and there found to take lead drive carry away and impound and in pound to detain and keep until the said several annual sums or yearly rent Charges above mentioned and all arrears of the same respectively so unpaid if any shall happen to be and all the costs charges and Expences attending the taking and keeping such Distress and Distresses shall be fully satisfied and paid and in default of payment in due time after such Distress or Distresses shall be so taken to appraise and sell or otherwise dispose of the same Distress and Distresses or otherwise to act therein according to Law to the intent that Morally they the said several Annuitants or their respective Assigns shall and may be fully paid and satisfied the said several Annuities or yearly Rent charges above mentioned and every part and parts thereof respectively. And all costs and expenses attending the recovery of the same and to and for the further use Intent and Purpose that in case the said several Annuities or yearly Rent Charges above mentioned or any of them or any part or parts of them or any of them shall at any time or times be behind or unpaid by the space of fifty Days next after the same shall respectively become due and payable as aforesaid. Then and so often (although no formal demand shall be made thereof or of the Arrears thereof it shall and may be lawfull to and for the several Annuitants and their respective Assigns during the respective lives of such Annuitants into and upon all and singular the said Hereditaments and Premises so charged and chargeable with the payment thereof respectively as aforesaid and into and upon every or any part thereof to enter and the Rents Issues and Profits thereof and of every part thereof to have receive and take to their and every of their own use until they and every of them shall thereby and therewith be fully paid and satisfied the said several Annuities or yearly Rent Charges above mentioned and every of them and every part thereof respectively and all arrears of the same and all such arrears as shall incur during the time that they the said several Annuitants or their respective Assigns shall by virtue of such Entry or Entries be in possession of the said Premises together with all such costs charges and Expences as shall be laid out sustained or occasioned by or by reason of nonpayment such possession when taken to be without Impeachment of Waste.

And as to for and concerning the said Manors Hereditaments and Premises so charged and chargeable with the payment of the said sum of six hundred pounds and of the said several Annuities And the said Powers and Remedies for the Recovery of the same respectively hereinbefore contained and subject thereto. To the use and behoof of the said William Burrell and John Claxton their Heirs and Assigns for and during the Term of the natural life of the said Levina Luther without Impeachment of Waste upon Trust nevertheless to pay or to permit and suffer her the said Levina Luther or her Assigns to receive and take the Rents Issues and Profits of all and singular the same Premises during her life to and for her own sole and separate use and benefit without being subject to the power control Debts or Engagements of her present or any after taken Husband. And from and immediately after the decease of the said Levina Luther Then as to for and concerning all and singular the same Manors Hereditaments and Premises so charged and chargeable as aforesaid To the use and behoof of the said Elizabeth Bull and Catherine Bull their Heirs and Assigns for ever and to be equally divided between them share and share alike as Tenants in common and not as joint Tenants and to and for no other use Intent or Purpose whatsoever.

And as to for and concerning the said capital sum of twelve thousand four hundred and fifty two pounds Bank Stock and the said Capital Sum of three thousand seven hundred and fifty pounds East India Stock and all such other Bank Stock and East India Stock as I may be possessed of or entitled to at the time of my decease so given and bequeathed to the said William Burrell and John Claxton their Executors Administrators and Assigns as aforesaid the same are respectively so given and bequeathed to them upon the Trusts and for the intents and purposes hereinafter mentioned and declared of and concerning the same (that is to say) upon Trust that they my said Trustees and the survivor of them and the Executors and Administrators of such survivor shall and do stand possessed of and interested in the same for the further and better securing the several Annuities or Yearly Rent Charges hereinbefore mentioned and such other Annuities or Yearly Rent Charges as I may by any Codicil or Codicils to this my Will give direct or appoint and for that purpose in case the Rents Issues and Profits of my Manors Hereditaments and real Estates in the said Counties of Devon and Cornwall chargeable with the said several Annuities or Yearly Rent Charges as aforesaid shall not be sufficient to pay and satisfy the said Annuities and each and every of them from time to time as the same shall respectively become due Then and in such case I do order and direct the said William Burrell and John Claxton and the survivor of them and the executors Administrators and Assigns of such survivor by and out of the Interest Dividends and Annual Produce of the said Bank Stock and East India Stock to pay and make good any such Deficiency and subject to and from and after full payment of all the said several Annuities.

Then upon Trust to pay all such Interest Dividends and Annual produce of the said Bank Stock and East India Stock as shall accrue thereon or arise therefrom during the natural lives of the said Annuitants or any of them unto such Person or Persons and for such purposes as the said Levina Luther shall from time to time notwithstanding her Coverture by Note or Writing under her hand direct or appoint. And in

Default of such direction or appointment into the proper hands of her the said Levina Luther from time to time for her own sole and separate use and benefit without being subject or liable to the power control Debts or Engagements of her present or any after taken Husband, and the Receipts of the said Levina Luther or of such person or persons to whom she shall from time to time so direct the same to be paid as aforesaid shall from time to time notwithstanding her Coverture be good discharges for so much of such Interest Dividends and Annual Produce as in such Receipts shall be expressed to be received and from and after the decease of all the said several Annuitants in case the said Levina Luther shall survive them.

Then upon Trust that they the said William Burrell and John Claxton and the survivor of them and the Executors Administrators and Assigns of such survivor shall and do transfer the principal or capital of all the said Bank Stock and East India Stock unto such person or persons and for such intents and purposes as she the said Levina Luther by any Deed or Writing under her Hand notwithstanding her coverture shall direct or appoint and in Default of such Direction or Appointment unto her the said Levina Luther her Executors Administrators and Assigns to and for her own proper and separate use and benefit exclusive of and without being subject to the power debts or control of the present or any after taken Husband. But in case the said Levina Luther shall happen to die in the lifetime of the said several Annuitants or in the lifetime of any of them Then (subject to and after payment of any such deficiency as aforesaid) upon Trust that they the said William Burrell and John Claxton and the survivor of them and the Executors Administrators or Assigns of such survivor shall and do transfer all the said Bank Stock and East India Stock unto the said Elizabeth Bull and Catherine Bull their Executors Administrators and Assigns to be equally divided between them share and share alike to and for their own use and benefit.

Provided always and my Mind and Will is that it shall and may be lawful to and for the said William Burrell and John Claxton and the survivor of them and the Heirs of such survivor during the life of the said Levina Luther (by and with the consent and approbation of the said Levina Luther signified in writing under her hand and seal but not otherwise) by Indenture under their Hands and Seals or the hand and seal of the survivor of them or his Heirs to Demise or Lease all or any of the Manors Messuages Lands Tenements and Hereditaments hereinbefore mentioned and hereby devised to them the said William Burrell and John Claxton their Heirs and Assigns in Trust for the said Levina Luther or her Assigns during her life as aforesaid (except the said Mansion House called the Grove and the Lands Tenements and Hereditaments at the Grove and in the Parish of Chiswick aforesaid) unto any Person or Persons for one two or three life or lives or for any term or number of years determinable upon one two or three life or lives and either in possession or in reversion or remainder so as upon every such lease the usual yearly Rent be reserved and made payable during the continuance thereof respectively. And so as that in all such Leases there be contained a Clause of Re-entry for nonpayment of the Rent or Rents to be thereby respectively reserved and that each such Lessee to whom such Lease or Leases shall be made shall seal and deliver a Counterpart of such Lease or Leases.

And I do hereby further declare my Mind and Will to be that my said Trustees and the survivor of them and the Heirs Executors and Administrators of such survivor shall be charged and chargeable only for so much and such of the said Trust Estates Monies and Premises as they and each of them shall respectively actually receive by virtue of this my Will and that the one of them shall not be answerable or accountable for the other of them nor for the Acts Deeds Receipts Neglects or Defaults of the other of them But each of them for his own Acts Deeds Receipts Neglects and Defaults only. And that they or either of them shall not be answerable for any Bank Banker Broker or Goldsmith with whom or in whose hands the said Trust Estate and Monies or any part thereof shall or may at any time or times be lodged or deposited for safe custody or otherwise in the Execution of the aforesaid Trusts nor shall they or any or either of them be answerable or accountable for any Defect or Insufficiency (either in respect of Title or otherwise) of any Security or Securities; in or upon which the said Trust Monies or any part thereof shall or may at any time or times be placed out or invested or for any other Misfortune Loss or Damage which may happen in the Execution of the Trusts hereby in them reposed unless the same shall happen by or through their own wilful neglect or defaults respectively.

And also that they the said Trustees and the survivor of them and the Heirs Executors and Administrators of such survivor and each and every of them shall and may by and out of the Trust Monies which shall come to their or any of their hands by virtue of or in pursuance of this my Will deduct and retain to and reimburse themselves respectively and also allow to each other all such costs charges and expences as they or any of them shall or may at any time or times pay sustain expend or be put unto in and about the Execution of the several Trusts hereby in them reposed or any of them or in any wise in Relation thereto.

And I constitute and appoint the said William Burrell and John Claxton joint Executors of this my Will and revoking all former Wills by me at any time heretofore made I publish and declare this only to be my last Will and Testament In Witness thereof I have hereunto set my hand and seal the twenty fourth day of July in the year of our Lord one thousand seven hundred and eighty two.

Humphrey Morice

Signed sealed published and declared by the said Humphrey Morice the Testator as and for his last Will and Testament in the presence of us who in his presence at his request and in the presence of each other have hereunto subscribed our Hands as Witnesses.

John Kerby, Stafford Street

Charles Youd, Stafford Street

Thomas Stone, Bond Street

[Continuation following the end of the Will of Humphrey Morice Esquire]

No. 1

Nice 10 Oct. 1782

Dear Sir

The Trust I have troubled you with in my Will is this: You and Mr Claxton my other Trustee and as well as yourself my Executor are to receive six hundred a year from my estates in Devon and Cornwall to pay for the maintenance of the horses and dogs I leave behind me and for the expence of servants to look after them besides Will Bishop the groom. He is I am persuaded very honest & will not let bills be brought in for any oats hay straw or tares more than have really been had. As the horses die off the overplus of monies expended on their account will increase and it is to be paid to Mrs Luther whom I have made my heir. Was she not circumstanced as she is I should never have thought of taking this precaution as I have an implicit confidence in her. She indeed desired annuities might be left to all the animals in my Will but I thought it better to make my intentions known to you by a private Letter as their being mentioned in my Will would perhaps be ridiculed after my death and though I should be ignorant of it and of course not care about it yet the friends I leave behind me might not like to hear it. Mrs Luther I am persuaded will never make any dispute about the bills you allow on the aforesaid account out of the said six hundred pounds a year nor will those that come after her when by this letter being read to them they are informed of my intentions.

I have left other annuities charged on my Devon & Cornish estates. If from the revenues of those estates they should some years not produce enough to satisfy the annuitants I have left Bank Stock etc in Trust to you and Mr Claxton to help pay the annuities.

I desire you to accept my repeating watch No. 17527, that Mr Claxton will accept the repeating watch No. 14580 and the repeater made by Julian Le Roy No. 2659 I desire you will give to Mrs Jane White of Gamlingay near Pothore [Potton] as it was left to me by her father Wm Henry Barnard Esqr. The other Repeater I have given away in my Will to my Servant Richard Deale No. 15129.

I consulted Mr Wilmot about the propriety of writing this letter. He approved of it and you will see my Will alludes to it.

The single stone brilliant ring kept in an ivory egg I desire Sir Wm Lee will accept and there is with it a burying ring of Mr Brown his great great uncle who lived to such an advanced age. My diamond shoe and knee buckles I mean to include in my wearing apparell left to Richard Deale, also gold headed canes, as his attention and fidelity increases every day and sorry I am to say he is the only servant I ever had who seemed sensible of good treatment and did not behave ungratefully.

I hope the Trust will not be a troublesome one to you except just at first. Pray excuse it. When you receive this I shall be no more but at the time of writing it I am my dear Sir most sincerely yours, H Morice
10 Oct 1782

[Second continuation following the end of the Will of Humphrey Morice Esquire]

This is the Will of me Humphrey Morice as far as relates to my effects here at Naples and is not meant in any manner to affect the Will I made just before I left England in July 1782 but may properly be called a Codicil to that Will.

I appoint my servant John Allan and my servant Richard Deale joint Executors of this my Will or Codicil being confident I can depend upon them for the taking care of my effects and of what I leave, that they will dispose of it as I order them by letter or otherwise also that they will render a faithfull account to the person who when my former Will is opened appears to be entitled to my effects. The said former Will not to be opened 'till their return to England.

I desire to be buried at Naples if I dye there and in a leaden coffin if such a thing is to be had. Just before it is Soldered I request the surgeon in Lord Tylney's house or some other surgeon may take out my heart or perform some other operation to ascertain my being really dead.

The five servants I brought with me from England to have a compleat suit of mourning. I mean for them to continue in the house I inhabit at Chiaya [Chiaia] 'till it is a proper season for them to return to England so as for them to avoid taking that journey during the extremes of winter or summer according to the time I may happen to die. Their maintenance here, also the expenses of their return to England to be paid out of my effects.

I desire my two Executors before they set out, to dispose of the furniture I bought of Count Rosamovssky [perhaps Count Andrey Rasumovsky, later Russian ambassador in Vienna] and of what other things I leave as I have directed them.

By my former Will my wearing apparell is given to my servant Richard Deale except watches rings and diamonds, this bequest having been made prior to my present Valet de Chambre coming to live with me. If he Richard Deale chuses it, he may dispose of the whole or part at Naples.

My servants to continue housekeeping from the time of my death to the time of their departure. And when they my two aforesaid Executors think proper to discharge any or all of the six servants I took at Naples to give each and all of such servants forty ounces each except Giovanni Bruscogloni to whom I give one hundred ounces or three hundred ducats and if he chuses to return to Florence the expences of his journey thither to be allowed him.

I have left drafts payable to John Allan and Richard Deale to defray present expenses. My next heir will send them what more be wanted by them, and to pay their journey home by land in the manner I have ordered.

I give to my servant John Bohm [?] one annuity or yearly sum of forty pounds of England to be paid in like manner as I have orderd sundry other annuities in my former Will and to be issuing and payable out of the same securities.

And confirming my former Will I have to this my second Will or Codicil set my hand and seal this fourteenth day of March in the year of our Lord one thousand seven hundred and eighty four.
Humphrey Morice
Signed sealed and declared by the said Humphrey Morice to be his second Will or Codicil to his former Will in the presence of us
Jos. Webb
Theo Luders
Thomas Pettingal
All three English gentlemen at present resident at Naples

[A paragraph in Italian has been added at the bottom, translated as follows]

I the undersigned, Chancellor for the British Nation at the Consulate General in the Kingdom of Naples, confirm that the signature is written in his own hand by Humphrey Morice, English gentleman, and the seal is his own seal.

Dr Libovio Scala, Chancellor

13th February 1786

Appeared personally William Burrell of Harley Street in the County of Middlesex Esquire and John Claxton of Shirley in the County of Surrey Esquire the Executors named in the last Will and Testament of the Right Honourable Humphrey Morice formerly of the parish of Chiswick in the County of Middlesex but late of the City of Naples Esquire deceased. And made oath that in the said Will of the said deceased bearing date the twenty fourth day of July in the year of our Lord one thousand seven hundred and eighty two there is contained in the first sheet or page thereof the following clause to wit: 'But as to my three other repeating Watches and all my Diamond Rings and Buckles I give and desire the same to be disposed of unto such persons and in such manner as I shall mention in a Writing or Letter that I shall leave with this my Will'. And that in the sixth sheet or page thereof is contained the following clause to wit: 'To the use Intent and purpose that they the said William Burrell and John Claxton and the survivor of them or the Heirs Executors or Administrators of such survivor shall and do in the first place by and out of the Rents Issues and Profits of the said several Manors Hereditaments and Premises deduct and set apart annually the sum of six hundred pounds and pay apply and dispose of the same unto such person or persons in such manner and for such purpose as I shall mention in a writing or Letter that I shall leave with this my Will at the time of my decease'. And these Deponents further jointly and severally depose that the paper writing hereunto annexed marked No. 1 beginning thus 'Nice 10 Oct 1782 Dear Sir The trust I have troubled you with in my Will is this' ending 'pray excuse it when you receive this I shall be no more but at the time of writing it I am my dear Sir most sincerely yours', and thus subscribed 'H. Morice' and again dated 'Nice 10 Oct 1782', which said paper writing or Letter was delivered to him this Deponent William Burrell in or about the month of November one thousand seven hundred and eighty five in an envelope or cover hereunto annexed marked No. 2 by Mr Bull at the desire of Mrs Luther the principal Legatee in the said Will, is the only paper of a Testamentary nature which has come to these Deponents Hands possession or knowledge save and except the aforesaid Will and a Codicil which is hereunto annexed bearing date the fourteenth day of March one thousand seven hundred and eighty

four, and a Duplicate of the aforesaid paper writing or Letter marked No. I
as aforesaid which was received by him the Deponent John Claxton at or
about the time aforesaid. And these Deponents lastly say that they were
well acquainted with the deceased and with his manner and character of
handwriting and subscription having often seen him write and subscribe
his name to writing and having now carefully viewed and perused the
said paper writing beginning ending subscribed and dated as aforesaid
they say that the same is all of the proper handwriting and subscription
of the said Humphrey Morice deceased

William Burrell

John Claxton

This same day the said William Burrell and John Claxton were duly sworn
to the truth of this affidavit before me George Harris, Surrogate.

This Will was proved at London with two Codicils the sixteenth day of
February in the year of our Lord one thousand seven hundred and eighty
six before the Worshipful George Harris Doctor of Laws, Surrogate of
the Right Worshipful Peter Calvert Doctor of Laws Master Keeper or
Commissary of the Prerogative Court of Canterbury lawfully constituted,
by the oaths of William Burrell and John Claxton Esquires the Executors
named in the said Will to whom Administration of all and singular the
Goods Chattels and Credits of the deceased was granted they having
been first sworn duly to administer power reserved of granting a Probate
of the second of the said Codicils to John Allan and Richard Deale the
Executors therein named limited to the deceased's Effects at Naples in
Italy when they or either of them shall apply for the same.

Appendix 5: Genealogical Tables

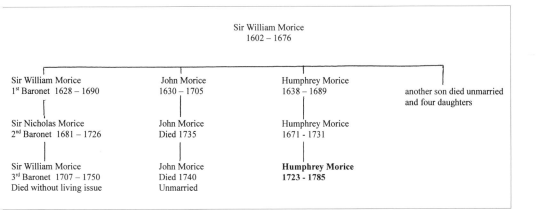

Sir William Morice
1602 – 1676

| Sir William Morice 1st Baronet 1628 – 1690 | John Morice 1630 – 1705 | Humphrey Morice 1638 – 1689 | another son died unmarried and four daughters |

Sir Nicholas Morice
2nd Baronet 1681 – 1726

John Morice
Died 1735

Humphrey Morice
1671 - 1731

Sir William Morice
3rd Baronet 1707 – 1750
Died without living issue

John Morice
Died 1740
Unmarried

Humphrey Morice
1723 - 1785

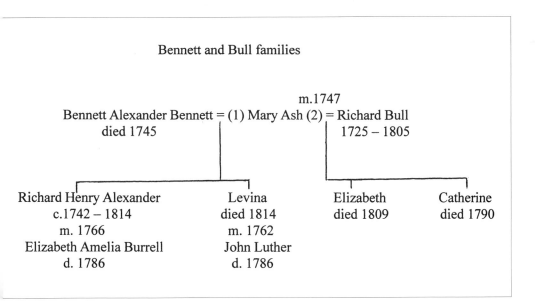

Bennett and Bull families

m.1747
Bennett Alexander Bennett = (1) Mary Ash (2) = Richard Bull
died 1745   1725 – 1805

| Richard Henry Alexander c.1742 – 1814 m. 1766 Elizabeth Amelia Burrell d. 1786 | Levina died 1814 m. 1762 John Luther d. 1786 | Elizabeth died 1809 | Catherine died 1790 |

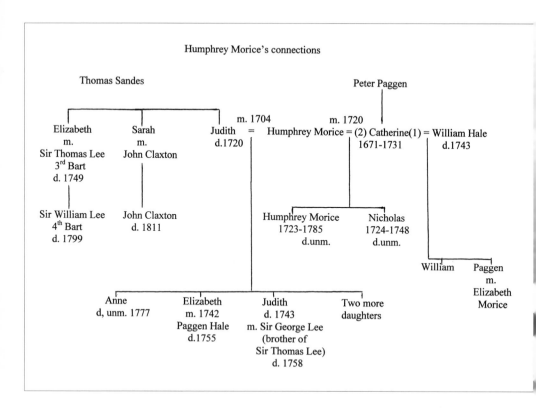

Humphrey Morice's connections

Notes

1 The Letters

1. Chiswick, 1801 Census, *A List returned of the Population of Chiswick Town and Parish in the County of Middlesex taken in the month of March 1801*, Local Studies Department, Chiswick Library.
2. Letter 9, 25 March 1784, note 8.
3. Will, p. 142; Letter 7, 26 January 1784.
4. Letter 15, 29 November 1784.
5. Devonshire Mss, Chatsworth, AS617.
6. *Book of Fees Paid for Baptisms Marriages and Burials, 1781–1792* (compiled by the vestry clerk), kept in the parish archives of St Nicholas church, Chiswick.
7. Letter 9, 25 March 1784.
8. Letter 3, 20 September 1783.
9. Letter 10, 29 April 1784; Letter 16, 4 February 1785; Letter 20, 12 September 1785.
10. Letter 12, 26 July 1784.
11. Letter 5, 30 November 1783.
12. Letter 6, 4 January 1784.
13. Letter 17, 4 April 1785.
14. Letter 13, 20 August 1784.
15. Letter 2, 25 August 1783, first fragment.
16. Letter 7, 26 January 1784.
17. Letter 6, 4 January 1784; Letter 7, 26 January 1784; Letter 9, 25 March 1784.
18. Letter 17, 4 April 1785; *Book of Fees Paid for Baptisms Marriages and Burials, 1781–1792* (compiled by the vestry clerk), kept in the parish archives of St Nicholas church, Chiswick.
19. Letter 8, 23 February 1784.
20. Letter 7, 26 January 1784; Letter 8, 23 February 1784; Letter 16, 4 February 1785.
21. Letter 9, 25 March 1784.
22. Will, p. 143.
23. Letter 3, 20 September 1783; Letter 12, 26 July 1784; Letter 14, 17 September 1784.
24. Letter 7, 26 January 1784.
25. Letter 1, 10 August 1783.
26. An ounce, or onza, was a Neapolitan coin worth perhaps ten shillings at the time; a ducat was also a Neapolitan coin worth three to the onza.
27. Letter 15, 29 November 1784.
28. Will, p. 129.
29. Letter 15, 29 November 1784.
30. For wages at this time see Hecht, J. Jean, *The Domestic Servant in Eighteenth Century England* (1980), pp. 142, 149; for board wages, p. 154.
31. From information kindly provided by Mr Fred Goatcher.

2 The Life of Humphrey Morice

Much of the information in this biography, if not otherwise footnoted, is based on the biographies in the *Oxford Dictionary of National Biography* and Namier, Lewis and Brooke, John *The History of Parliament, The House of Commons 1754–1790* (1964).

1. Northumberland Archives, Woodhorn, ZSW 554/19, 20, 37.

2. See for example the fragment enclosed with Letter 19, 1 September 1785.

3. See page 18.

4. Lysons, Daniel, *Environs of London, Volume Two: Middlesex* (1795), p. 197.

5. Letter from Humphrey Morice to Sir William Lee, 5 December 1768, Centre for Buckinghamshire Studies, D/LE/D/8/19.

6. Letter from Horace Walpole to Sir Horatio Mann, 20 August 1782, Lewis, W. S. (ed.) *The Yale Editions of Horace Walpole's Correspondence*, 1937-1983, Vol 25, p.37.

7. *Charity School Subscriptions 1774–1790*, booklet held in the parish archives at St Nicholas church, Chiswick.

8. Letter from Sir Horatio Mann to Horace Walpole, 20 October 1760 in Lewis, W. S. (ed.), *The Yale Editions of Horace Walpole's Correspondence* (1937–1983), Vol. 25, p. 442.

9. Letter from Horace Walpole to the Countess of Upper Ossory, 22 June 1779 in Lewis, W. S. (ed.), *The Yale Editions of Horace Walpole's Correspondence* (1937–1983), Vol. 33, p. 104.

10. Letter from Horace Walpole to the Countess of Upper Ossory, 21 July 1782 in Lewis, W. S. (ed.), *The Yale Editions of Horace Walpole's Correspondence* (1937–1983), Vol. 33, pp. 297–8.

11. Letter from Sir Horatio Mann to Horace Walpole, 10 October 1783 in Lewis, W. S. (ed.), *The Yale Editions of Horace Walpole's Correspondence* (1937–1983), Vol. 25, p. 435.

12. Letter 17, 4 April 1785.

13. Letter from Horace Walpole to the Countess of Upper Ossory, 17 November 1784 in Lewis, W. S. (ed.), *The Yale Editions of Horace Walpole's Correspondence* (1937–1983), Vol. 33, p. 452.

14. Northumberland Archives, Woodhorn, ZSW 554/47.

15. Devonshire Mss, Chatsworth, L50/9/16, p. 4.

16. Pinkerton, J. M., 'Richard Bull of Ongar Essex', *The Book Collector*, 27 (1) (1978), p. 46.

17. Letter 3, 20 September 1783, note 9.

18. Letter from Kitty Clive to Humphrey Morice, 10 December 1761, Northumberland Archives, Woodhorn, ZSW 554/13.

19. Letter 10, 29 April 1784; Letter 16, 4 February 1785.

20. See page 144.

21. See illustration 3.

22. Toynbee, Paget (ed.), 'Walpole's Journals of Visits to Country Seats', *Journal of the Walpole Society*, 16 (1927–28), pp. 77–78.

23. Northumberland Archives, Woodhorn, ZSW 554/53, 54.

24. Trumbach, Randolph, 'Sex, Gender and Sexual Identity in Modern Culture', *Journal of the History of Sexuality*, 2, p. 188; *The Trial of Samuel Grimshaw and John Ross*, Old Bailey Proceedings, 17 July 1759, pamphlet published by M. Cooper.

25. Colman, George, *Random Records* (1830), p. 280; Devonshire Mss, Chatsworth, 1811 inventory of Chiswick House.

26. Letter 8, 23 February 1784.

27. See page 142.

28. Letter 15, 29 November 1784, note 7.

29. See Appendix 4.

30. Northumberland Archives, Woodhorn, ZSW 554/50; ZSW 554/51.

31. See page 143.

32. See illustration 14.

3 The Grove Estate from the Beginning to 1775

1. *Calendar of Close Rolls, Henry IV*, Vol. 4 (1409–1413), p. 334; *Victoria County History of Middlesex*, Vol. 7, p. 76.
2. *Churchwardens' Rates and Accounts, 1636–1663*, St Nicholas church, Chiswick. See also Devonshire Mss, Chatsworth, L21/31, f. 4 (in a survey of the manor of Sutton Court of 1664).
3. *Victoria County History of Middlesex*, Vol. 7, p. 76.
4. Devonshire Mss, Chatsworth, L50/9/29, 'Abstract of the Title of the Reverend Eyre Harrington Devisee In Trust under the Will of the Rev Robert Louth deceased to the Capital Messuage Park etc called The Grove Chiswick in the County of Middlesex', pp. 1–8.
5. Devonshire Mss, Chatsworth, L50/9/29, pp. 9–12. The earl has sometimes been confused with Thomas Robinson, Baron Grantham.
6. Devonshire Mss, Chatsworth, L50/9/16, 'Abstract of the Title of the Reverend Eyre Harrington Devisee In Trust under the Will of the Rev Robert Louth deceased to the Capital Messuage Park etc called The Grove Chiswick in the County of Middlesex', pp. 1–5.
7. Devonshire Mss, Chatsworth, L50/9/16, pp. 5–6.
8. Devonshire Mss, Chatsworth, L50/9/16, pp. 8–9, 11, 13.

4 The Estate Bought by Humphrey Morice

1. The description of the estate is collated with the deed itself, dated 4 February 1777. Devonshire Mss, Chatsworth, L50/9/8, and relevant part of L50/9/16, p. 6.
2. See the various series of rentals in the Devonshire Mss, Chatsworth; Devonshire Mss, Chatsworth, L16/7, 'Freehold parcels in the Conveyance of Barker's Estate at Chiswick, 1763'; *Victoria County History of Middlesex*, Vol. 7, p. 77.
3. Crowther letter, Local Studies Collection, Chiswick Library; Draper, Warwick, *Chiswick* (1923), pp. 144–5; Wisdom, James, 'Grove House', *Brentford and Chiswick Local History Society Journal*, 3 (1982), p. 17; Phillimore, W. P. W. and Whitear, W. H., *Historical Collections Relating to Chiswick* (1897), p. 13 quoting John Bowack, from his *Antiquities of Middlesex* (1705–6), p. 275.
4. Devonshire Mss, Chatsworth, L65/11; *House Beautiful*, February 1920, pp. 108–9. The plans were drawn by Charles Edward Hodge in 1889 and show a proposed addition to the house. See illustrations 29 and 30.
5. Lysons, Daniel, *Environs of London, Volume Two: Middlesex* (1795), p. 197.
6. Devonshire Mss, Chatsworth, L65/11.
7. Hodge, *op. cit.*; illustrations 29 and 30.
8. Bowack, quoted in Phillimore and Whitear, p. 13; *The Tours of John Loveday of Caversham, 1728 to 1765*, 'Tour 97, 24 August 1744', see www.johnlovedayofcaversham.co.uk.
9. Letters 5 and 15; Lysons, p. 197.

5 The Grove Estate from 1785 to the End

1. Northumberland Record Office, Woodhorn, ZSW 554/50; Pinkerton, *op cit*, p. 46.
2. Devonshire Mss, Chatsworth, L50/9/16, pp. 11–12, 13–14.
3. Devonshire Mss, Chatsworth, L50/9, pp. 14, 15.
4. Devonshire Mss, Chatsworth, L50/9, p. 18. This part of the deed was registered in June 1807.
5. Devonshire Mss, Chatsworth, L50/9, pp. 16–24.
6. Mrs Luther's will, PROB 11/1653; Devonshire Mss, Chatsworth, L50/9/16, pp. 25–32, 33–34, 35, 36.
7. Colman, George, *Random Records* (1830), p. 289; Lowth's will, PROB 11/1661.
8. Devonshire Mss, Chatsworth, L50/9/16, p. 35.
9. Devonshire Mss, Chatsworth, L50/9/16, pp. 36, 37.

10. Devonshire Mss, Chatsworth, L21/1, a plan of land for sale and the estate marked out for roads for the 'villas'.

11. *Morning Press*, Saturday 11 June, also *Standard* for the same date.

12 Devonshire Mss, Chatsworth, L65/11. The description of the estate from the auction document is printed above, pp. 115; Devonshire Mss, Chatsworth L50/13/1 and 50/13/9, 'The Conveyance of the Grove Estate to the Duke of Devonshire'; L50/9/16.

13. Devonshire Mss, Chatsworth, L21/12, a series of rentals covering 1806 to 1814; L16/20, rentals from 1817. Jessop may have taken over Warren Wall field by 1826, see Devonshire Mss, Chatsworth, L21/13; *Churchwardens' Rates and Accounts, 1821–1856*, St Nicholas church, Chiswick.

14. Devonshire Mss, Chatsworth, L16/20; Colvin, H. M., *A Biographical Dictionary of British Architects, 1600–1840* (2008), p. 173. For the reduction in size of the Grove, see illustrations 5 and 27.

15. Devonshire Mss, Chatsworth, L21/13, rental for 1837; L82/4, rental for 1844.

16. Devonshire Mss, Chatsworth, L82/4, rentals 1843 and 1844; Chiswick Rate Books, Local Studies Collection, Chiswick Library.

17. Wisdom, James and Bott, Val, 'Col. Shipway's Pedigree', *Brentford and Chiswick Local History Journal*, 5 (1996), p. 17; Draper, Warwick, *Chiswick* (1923), p. 144.

18. Harris, John, *Moving Rooms* (2007), pp. 190–1; Metropolitan Museum of Art Accession Nos 31.92.35 and 32.106.28. For the fireplace, see illustration 28.

Appendix 1

For all Members of Parliament in this appendix see the biographies in Namier, Lewis and Brooke, John *The History of Parliament, The House of Commons 1754–1790* (1964).

1. Essex Record Office, D/DQ 41/258. This record must be dated between 1750 when Morice became 'of Werrington' and 1785 when he died; Cornwall Record Office, G/1161/1, 2.

2. Pinkerton, J. M., 'Richard Bull of Ongar, Essex', *The Book Collector*, 27 (1) (1978), p. 46.

3. Pinkerton, p. 47.

4. Farrant, John H., 'The Family Circle and Career of William Burrell, Antiquary', *Sussex Archaeological Collections*, 139 (2001), pp. 169–85.

5. Will of Benjamin Ash, PROB 11/632.

6. Namier, Lewis and Brooke, John, *op. cit.*, 2 (1964), pp. 130–1, under Bull.

7. Pinkerton, p. 42; Anon, *Anecdotes of the Life of Richard Watson, Bishop of Llandaff* (1817), pp. 27–8.

8. Will of John Luther, PROB/11/1137.

9. Pinkerton, p. 45; Northumberland Archives, Woodhorn, ZSW 554/49, 554/96.

10. Assignment of mortgage, Cornwall Record Office, P185/28/1.

11. Centre for Buckinghamshire Studies, D-LE/D/8/1–8.

12. Letter 7, 26 January 1784.

Appendix 2

1. From numbers 235 and 242 in the forthcoming catalogue of Batoni's paintings by Edgar Peters Bowron and Peter Bjorn Kerber, to be published by Yale University Press with the support of the Paul Mellon Centre for Studies in British Art. We are most grateful to Dr Bowron for letting us see a section from his manuscript in advance of publication.

2. Thanks are due to Sir James Graham for sending us a copy of his unpublished article written at the time of the Batoni exhibition in 2008.

3. Bowron and Kerber; Centre for Buckinghamshire Studies, Lee Papers, D/LE/D/8/19, 8/20, 8/21.

4. Bowron and Kerber, picture no. 241.

Select Bibliography

Baker, T. F. T. and Elrington, C. R. (eds), *Victoria County History of Middlesex*, Vol. 7 (1982).

Baker, T.H., *Records of the Seasons; Prices of Agricultural Produce and Phenomenon Observed in the British Isles* (1883).

Beverley, Sir William, *Prices and Wages from the Twelfth Century to the Nineteenth Century* (1939).

Draper, Warwick, *Chiswick* (1923).

Farrant, John H., 'The Family Circle and Career of William Burrell, Antiquary', *Sussex Archaeological Collections*, 139 (2001), pp. 169–85.

Goldman, L. (ed.), *Oxford Dictionary of National Biography* (2001–4 and online).

Hecht, J. Jean, *The Domestic Servant in Eighteenth Century England* (1980).

Hill, Bridget, *Servants: English Domestics in the Eighteenth Century* (1996).

Lysons, Daniel, *Environs of London, Volume Two: Middlesex* (1795).

Musson, Jeremy, *Up and Down Stairs: The History of the Country House Servant* (2009).

Namier, Lewis and Brooke, John, *The History of Parliament, The House of Commons 1754–1790* (1964 and online).

Phillimore, W. P. W. and Whitear, W. H., *Historical Collections Relating to Chiswick* (1897).

Pinkerton, J. M., 'Richard Bull of Ongar, Essex', *The Book Collector*, 27 (1) (1978), pp. 41–59.

Richardson, R. C., *Household Servants in Early Modern England* (2010).

Steedman, Carolyn, *Labours Lost: Domestic Service and the Making of Modern England* (2009).

Stratton, J. M. and Whitlock, Ralph, (ed.), *Agricultural Records, AD 22–1968* (1969).

Thorold Rogers, J. E., *A History of Agriculture and Prices in England*, Vol. 7, Part 1 (1902).

Acknowledgements

Firstly thanks are due to the London Borough of Hounslow for allowing access to the collection of letters which form the basis of this book and for permission to publish them, and to those members of the Brentford & Chiswick Local History Society who made the initial transcriptions of the letters, as follows: Hugh Cochrane, the late Ted Crouchman, Christine Hall, Janet McNamara, Mary Pickford, Jeanne Whitby and Sheila Wheatcroft, but above all to the late Mary King, who in addition to transcribing some of the letters herself checked the rest and typed out two sets, one in the original spelling and layout and one in a more modernised format and spelling. She also painstakingly went through the letters, taking out all the names and setting them in context with quotations from the letters. These lists have been invaluable. She also transcribed the very long and complex will of Humphrey Morice, an enormous, invaluable and difficult task.

We would also like to thank the archives staff at Chatsworth, that is Diane Naylor, Stuart Band, Andrew Peppitt and James Towe, who over many years have patiently retrieved for us countless documents in their care on which parts of this book are based.

We owe great thanks to our friend the late Philip Daykin for putting his extensive knowledge of veterinary medicine at our disposal and for taking a personal interest in the project and to the late Dr Frank Rackow for his comments on the human illnesses described in the letters.

We also want to thank Val Bott for information on Frances Gray mustard seed seller, and for allowing us to use her copy of the *House Beautiful* article containing the plan of Grove House, and her and James Wisdom for their interest in this project over the past ten years; Mr Fred Goatcher for explaining the postal marks on the letters and the route the letters would have taken; Sir James Graham for sending us a copy of his unpublished article on his portrait of Humphrey Morice; Dr Edgar Peters Bowron for allowing us to see and use drafts of his forthcoming catalogue of Pompeo Batoni's paintings by himself and Dr Peter Bjorn Kerber; Wandsworth Parks Department for giving us access to the Huguenot burial ground at Wandsworth to photograph the Paggen tomb, Wandsworth Heritage Services for giving us a transcript of the inscription on the tomb, Doreen Leach for information on the doctors and the Lock Hospital, and Cris Reay for seeking a document in the Northumberland Archives at Woodhorn.

Thanks are due to Sir James and Lady Graham of Norton Conyers for allowing us to reproduce their portrait of Humphrey Morice; to Wadsworth Atheneum Museum of Art and Art Resource NY for the head-and-shoulders portrait of Humprey Morice; to the Harris Museum and Art Gallery, Preston, Lancashire and the Bridgeman Art Library for the Arthur Devis Bull family group and to the Lewis Walpole Library, Yale University for the picture of the footman.

Thanks are also due to James Marshall of the Local Studies Collection, Chiswick Library and to Vanda Foster at Gunnersbury Park Museum for allowing us to use pictures from their collections.

Index

Some illustrations are indexed with a number and an asterisk

Ague, 40, 41
Ale and beer, 12, 24
Allan, Charlotte, bequest, 96, 132
Allan, Hannah, bequest, 96, 133
Allan, John, 'the younger', 46, bequest, 96, 132, 133, 136, 137
Allan, John, 28, 31, 43, 62, 74, bequest, 135, 137, executor for Naples will, 15, 143, his room, 13, 43, payment of bills, 9
Amelia, Princess, 94, 96
Animal fund at the Grove, 18, 142-143
Arbbale tree, see Poplar tree
Asafoetida, 43, 46
Ash, Benjamin, 122, 124
Ash, Mary, 122, 124
Asses milk, 25
Association against robbery, see Chiswick Association
Auckland, John, 10, 40, Association against robbery, 73, 75, payment to, 52, request for tithes, 76, 78

Ball, William, bills, 49, 50, 62
Barker family, owners of the Grove, 111-112,
Barker, Anthony, 111
Barker, Henry, sale of the Grove, 111-112
Barker, Scorie, 111
Barkers Rails, damage to, 47, 50
Barley, spent, horse feed, 68
Barnard, William Henry, 143
Batoni, Pompeo, 126
Bear Key market, 32, 34
Bedford, Duke of, 95
Beniworth, Joseph, corn dealer and baker, bills, 27, 30, 66, 84, 85, draft for, 85
Bennett, Bennett Alexander, 122
Bennett, Richard Henry

Alexander, family, 122, friend of Morice, 95, trustee for the Grove, 118
Bishop, James, 72, 74
Bishop, Will 6, claims was not at home, 43, death, 10, his job, 9-10, letters written by 8, livery, 37, money sent to, 85, possible wage, 52, 53, problem with dates, 57, slanders about, 43, 45, suggestion to hire a helper for him, 48, 50, trustworthiness, 10, 142
Blake, Charles, tinsmith, 44, 76
Board wages, 12, 16-17, draft for, 62, payments, 72-73
Bodenham, John, bills for hats, 44, 46, 49, 50, 62
Boham, John, bequest, 144, his room, 13, 15, in Italy, 15
Bolden, John, agreement for following year, 73,bill for hay, straw and tares, 73, 75, draft for money, 79, 81, farmer, 33, wants money on account, 66
Borsley, Joseph Atkins, tenant of the Grove, 121
Bowack , John, 6, 116
Bowlden, see Bolden
Bradworthy, Devon, 135
Bread and beef, Christmas, 40
Brentford, 23, 32
Broad Clyst, Devon, 135
Broken windedness, in horses, 48, 50
Brown, John, 61
Bruscoglioni, Giovanni, Morice's valet in Naples, 15, 16, 99, 144
Bull, Catherine and Elizabeth, Morice's residuary legatees, 95, 99, visit Grove, 60
Bull, Catherine, 122, 125, bequest, 130, 139, 140, residuary legatee, 117
Bull, Elizabeth, 122, 125, bequest, 130, 139, 140, residuary legatee, 117

Bull, Richard, 16, 46, 117, 124, bequest, 129-130, family and life, 122-123, friend of Morice, 95, letter about puppy, 61, payment of bills, 9, picture of, illustration 2*, report on Morice's health, 84, trustee for Morice, 112, visits Grove, 60, 70, 84
Burglary attempt, 65
Burrell, Elizabeth Amelia, 122
Burrell, Peter, 122, 123
Burrell, Sir William, 95, 99, bequest, 133, 143, executor for Morice, 123, executor, letter to, 142
Burton Decimus, 120
Burton, Septimus, tenant of the Grove, 120
Butter receipts, 52, 53
Bye, Robert, 43, 45
Byways, see Highways

Calomel, 27, 30, 33
Camelford, Lord, 99
Canker, in horses, 46
Captain, dog, 21
Cart horses, buying, 40, 41
Carter, Robert, accused of fathering a child, 11, 55-56, 58, 64, 87, 88, advance on wages, 76, 77, asks for time off, 52, date of year end, 63, illnesses, 66, 83, 86, letter to Morice, 56, 87-88, money received, 52, Morice's generosity to, 96, new clothes, 37, seeks Morice's advice, 63, stable hand, 10, 11, teetotal claim, 12
Cattle on estate, 37, 40, 52, 53
Chandler, Mary, 32, 49, bill received, 37, payment for bill, 47
Chauldron, of coal, 38
Chestnuts and walnuts, sale of, 37, 38, 73, 75, 116
Chichester, Sir John, visits the Grove, 80, 81

Chipstead, Surrey, 99, 130

Chiswick Association for
Prosecuting Thieves, 73, 75, 103*

Chiswick, bequest to poor
of parish, 132, building of
workhouse, 84, 86, deaths in, 78

Chiswick workhouse, 84, 86

Christmas bread and beef, 40

Chroust, Henry, see Cross

Church lecture, 84, 86

Church lecturer, 66, 68

Church rates, 27, 55, 58

Claxton, John, 99, 117, bequest,
130, 133, 143, executor for
Morice, 15, 95, 123-124, executor,
letter to, 142

Clive, Kitty. actress, 96

Clyster, 46,

Clysters, bathing, 43

Coal, 36, 48, 49, 62, 79

Cocky, dog, 33, 35, 36, 40, 51, 55,
57, 62, 66, 73, 76, 79, 83

Coffin, Mr, visits the Grove,
80, 81

Collett, Thom, 22

Colman, George, visits the Grove,
98

Commin cordial balls, see Cumin

Constable, John, Churchwarden
of Wandsworth, 76

Cooper's bill, 54, 57

Cordial ball, 33, 35, 40

Corn buying, 32, 33

Corn market, Mark Lane, 32, 34

Corney House, 50, 91, 94, picture
of, illustration 8*

Cotton, John, Vestry Clerk, 28,
30, Christmas box, 67, 84, 86

Cowan, Dr, tenant of the Grove,
120

Cross, Henry, 29, 34, annual
wage, 82, clothes, 40, date of
year end, 63, money received,
53, new boots, 67, new hat, 37,
quarrels with Elizabeth Roberts,
22, spelling of name, 52, stable
hand, 10, venereal disease, 28

Cumin cordial balls, 33, 35, 40

Curate's lecture, 28, 30, 66, 67,
68, 84, 86

Currey, Benjamin, agent of the
Duke of Devonshire, 119

Curtis William, doctor, 28, 44, 51,
53, 55, 57, 76

Cutty, dog, 21

D'Arblay, Fanny, 125

Dancer, Thomas, Surveyor of the
Highways, 55, 58, 78

Deale, Mrs, 14, illness, 49, 52,
new lodgings, 84,86. Mrs Deale
sends her remembrances to Mr
Morice and Richard Deale at the
end of every letter.

Deale, Richard, bequests to, 99-

100, 129, 143, 135-136, 37, 144,
executor for Naples will, 15, 143,
good behaviour, 99, illness, 44,
letter from, 71, valet, 14-15

Denyer, Thomas, maltster, 32, 67,
bill for malt and bean, barley, 80

Devonshire, Duke of, 31, 111, buys
some of Grove land, 114, buys
the Grove, 119, sells the Grove,
120

Diamond, horse, 59

Dog, a dog, 61

Dog, strange, 21

Dogs, see Captain, Cocky, Cutty,
Dog, Flippant, Flora, Jully,
Phyllis, Ranger, Rattler, Snap,
Toper, Toss, Truelad, Twister

Drew, Mr, 25

Duncan, Lady Mary, writes to the
Bull sisters, 99

Editorial procedure, 19

Elder ointment, 65, 66, 67

Elliott, Sir William and Lady,
tenants of the Grove, 112

Emperor, horse, 36

Female staff numbers at the
Grove, 13

Fence, broken, 66

Finances, at the Grove, 16-20

Fits, in dogs, 30

Flippant, dog, 21, 62, 66

Flora, dog, 21

Ford, Sir Brinsley, 127

Foundling Hospital, bequest, 95,
132, Morice a subscriber to, 95

Fowl disease, see Venereal disease

Frances, John, blacksmith, bills,
28, 55, 66, 72, 76

Gale, great, 87

Game, Mr, enquiry after Morice,
74, 75

Gamlingay, Cambs, 143

Genny Cammil, see Jenny Camile

Gillman, gray horse, 43,
sandcrack, 55, 57

Goble, Mr, payment needed,
83, 85

Gould, Edward, maltster, 44, 67

Gould, William, annual wage,
82, date of year end, 62, money
received, 52, needs new boots,
67, new hat, 37, report on
quarrel, 22, stable hand, 10,

Grantham, Earl of, buys the
Grove, 112, lays out Grove
garden, 116, owner of the Grove,
93

Gray, Frances, seeds woman, bill,
37, 38, 76

Greenfield, James, bequest,
136-137

Greenwich, Parish, 56, Parish

overseers, 63, 87

Greville-Nugent, Fulke, 127

Grove animals, estates to provide
upkeep, 135, 142

Grove estate, annual stable
expenditure, 18, arrangements
for ownership after 1785, 117-
118, changes made by Earl of
Grantham, 112, description of,
113, early history, 111, gardens,
116, left to Levina Luther, 99,
Lowth mortgages on, 118, 119,
map in 1847, 104*, reduced in
size, 120, sale in 1775, 112, sale in
1831, 119, walnut and chestnut
trees, 37, 38, 73, 75, 116

Grove House, demolition, 121,
description of, 114-115, fireplace,
121, fragments of staircases, 121,
stables, 116

Gunnersbury, 94, 96, picture of,
illustration 7*

Gurney, Richard, tenant of the
Grove, 120

Hadley, Moses, 76, 78

Halwell, Devon, 135

Hammersmith, 59

Hankins, John, 30, 70, 73, clothes,
40, date of year end, 63, illness,
11, 51, 53, 55, 61, 63, 66, 68,
73, 76, 80, mother, 76, 79, 81,
replacement, 69, 72, stable hand,
10, 11

Harrington, Rev, James, 118, 119

Harris, Richard, 'the son', bequest,
136, 137

Harris, Richard, servant, 15,
bequest, 136, 137

Hasty, old horse, death, 59

Hay making, 62, 69, 83

Helston, John, 80, 81

Hern, Joseph, bill, 77

Hickman, Thomas, carter, 47, 49,
59, 60

Hicks Hall, 70, 71

Highways rate, 55, 62, 72, 76

Hill, John and Sarah, 112, 113

Hogarth House, 121

Hole, Mr, visits the Grove, 80, 81

Holgill, Thomas, 111

Holmes, John, bill, 27, 70, 71

Horn, Joseph, 44

Horse tax, 73, 74

Horses, see Diamond, Emperor,
Gillman, Hasty, Jenny Cammile,
Lady Thigh, Little John, Nero,
Nickey, Oronooko, Princess,
Rose, Silver, Slamekin, Smiler,
Spritely, Sultan, Tack, Tartar,
Whitefoot

House tax, 55, 57, 76, 78

Ice in Thames, 47

Iron spikes, theft, 73, 75, 79, 81

Italian servants at Naples, 16, bequest, 144
Italy, English staff in, 14-15

James powder, 40, 42, 44, 66
James, Henry, glazier, bill, 44, 55, 62
Jane, see Powers, Jane
Jenkins, Mr, 25
Jennings, Mr, tailor, 29
Jenny Camile, great bay mare, 33, 36, 87
Joye, Elizabeth, mortgagee for Morice, 112
Jullion, John, clockmaker, bill, 27, 39, 52, 76
Jully, dog, 51, 55, 61
Junice, horse, 33, 42, 45, 48, 83
Justice, eighteenth century, 34

Kemp, Mrs, 96
Kent, Henry, Morice's godson, 96, bequest, 136, 137
Kent, Joseph, 136
Kerby, John, Morice's agent, 16, 19, 27, 30, 42, drafts from, 75, 84, witness to Morice's will, 142, written to, 72
King, Lieutenant, 69, 71
Kingston market, 32

Lady Thigh, grey mare, 73, 76, 79, 83
Lamb, Justice, local JP, 32
Land tax, 56, 58, lowered, 84, 86, payment, 62-63, 72
Lausanne 8, 25
Lee, Sir George, 124
Lee, Sir Thomas, 124
Lee, Sir William, 124, owned portrait of Morice, 127
Leroy, Julian, watchmaker, 39, 41, 143
Letters, annotations, 8, , physical appearance, 18-19, postal costs, 19, provenance, 8
Library steps, broken, 51
Light, Ann, tailor, 84
Light, Mr, tailor, bill, 84, 86
Little John, horse, 33, 36
Little Petherick, Cornwall, 135
Lock Hospital, 11, 28, 30, 34, 95
Loveday, John, 116
Lowth family, state of finances, 119, 120
Lowth, Rev. Robert, buys the Grove, 118, death, 118,
Luders, Theo., 144
Luffincott, Devon, 135
Luther, John, 122, 124, 125
Luther, Levina, 122, bequests to, 133-134, 138-139, 139-140, death, 118, inherits the Grove, 95, 117, life and character, 124-125, picture of, illustration 2*, sale

of the Grove, 118, trust in by Morice, 142
Lying in Hospital for unmarried women, 95, bequest, 132
Lysons, Daniel, 38, 93, 115, 116

Macartney, Lord, 91
Mark Lane, 32
Marratt, Mr, supplier of oats, 32, bill for oats, 69, 70, 80, 81, bills to be sent to Morice, 72
Marshes powder, 40, 66
Marshgate, 21, 22
Mary Denford, horse, 33
Mary, ex servant, 43, 45
Maxwell, John, postmaster, 29, 31, 66, 84, 86
Mercury, metallic, 45
Merstham, Surrey, 99, 130
Millico, Guiseppi, 125
Moffett, Mr, Overseer of the Poor, 84, 86
Molesworth, Sir John, 86, 127
Molesworth, William, 85, 86
Montrose, Duchess of, enquires after Morice, 34, 35, 76, 78
Moreton Hall, staff size, 9
Morgan, Frances, carpenter, bill, 28, 77
Morice family tomb, 68-69, 70, 77
Morice, Anne, sister of Humphrey Morice, 43, 45, 62, 125, death, 64, servants, 45
Morice, Barbara, 127
Morice, Humphrey 8, animal lover, 96-97, 98, annuities in will, 99-100, arbitrator, 92, art lover 96, 97, as man of business, 92, 93, bequests to dependents, 96, birth, 90, blackmailed, 96, burial in Naples, 100, buys the Grove, 112, changes to the Grove, 93, character, 92, considerate to friends, 98, considerate to servants, 96, death, 100, education, 90, falls backwards down stairs, 79, 80, family, 90, family grave, 69, 70, 76, 78, picture of, illustration 14*, father, 90, , financial notes, 85, 86, fund for animals, 117, generosity, 95, 96, gifts to charities, 95, health, 24, 29, 44, 51, 52, 63, 67, 75, 79, 80, 84, 93, 94, life at the Grove, 93, pictures of, illustrations 1*, 3*, political career, 91-92, popularity, 94, 94-95, possibly homosexual, 96, purchase of the Grove, 93, request to be buried in family tomb, 100, 129, size of estate, 114, social life, 94-95, wealth, 98, will, 98-99, will at Naples, 143
Morice, Judith, 124
Morice, Sir William, Morice's

cousin, 91, 96
Mortlake, 32
Mozzi, Cavaliere Guilio, 92
Mulliner, Col. Robert, tenant of the Grove, 120

Naples 8, 25
Nero, horse, 83
Newcastle, Lord, 124
Newman, Timothy, Land tax collector, 55
Nickey, horse, 23, 28, 40, death, 43
Nice, 25
Norbon, Mr, dog vet, 43
Northcott, Devon, 135

Oats buying, 32, 34, high price, 48, price of, 42, 50-51, 69-70, 72, 74, 80
Opodeldoc, see Steers opodeldoc
Orford, Countess of, 92
Ormskirk powder, 21, 22
Oronooko, horse, 54, 87
Overseers of the Poor, 33, 35, 80

Packhorse inn, 59
Paggen family tomb, 68-69, 70, 77, 100, picture of, plate, 14*
Paggen, Peter, Morice's grandfather, 90
Paine, Ann, 25
Perigal, watchmaker, 39, 41
Peshall, Samuel, Rev., church lecturer, 68
Pettingal, Thomas, 144
Phillips, Charles, 124
Phillips, Elizabeth, old servant of Anne Morice, 45, illness, 43, 77, not well, 80
Phyllis, dog, 21, 47, 55
Pigeons, feed, 54, 57
Pitt, William, 61, 63
Poor Law, 35
Poor rate, 33, 35, 42, 55, 80, 84, not fixed, 52, payment, 72, settled, 70, 71
Poplar tree, blown down, 87
Porter, see Vickers, Joseph
Potton, Cambs, 143
Power, Jane, housekeeper, 14, 43, 46, 48, bequest, 136, 137, illness, 75
Princess, black mare, 66, 70
Prowett, Robert, tenant of the Grove, 120
Pullings, Elizabeth, bill, 27, 66, 84
Pullman, family, tenants and owners of the Grove, 120, 121
Puppy, lost, 59-60, found again, 61
Putrid fever, 77, 78

Quarrels in kitchen, 13, 21, 22, 34

Rabies, fear of, 21, 23

Ranger, Bishop's dog, 28, 33, 43, death, 51

Rattler, dog, 21

Razumovsky, Count Andrei, 144

Reeds, theft of, 32

Reeve, Albinia, bequest, 130

Reeve, Ann, bequest, 130

Reeve, Jane, bequest, 130

Reynolds, Catherine, old servant of Anne Morice, 43, 45

Richins, Mr, vet, 44, 54, 57, 59, 77

Richmond, Surrey, 32

Ridgeway, George Spencer, tenant of the Grove, 120

Right of Settlement, 58

Roberts, Elizabeth, cook, 13, 34, 43, 46, 66, bequest, 136, 137, death and funeral, 79, 80, illnesses, 13-14, 40, 43, 49, 51, lameness, 61, 76, new room for, 43, quarrels with Stable staff, 13, 21, 22

Rockingham, Marchioness of, 28, 30-31

Rose, chestnut mare, 36

Row, junior, 34, 35, 71, 74, 77, 78

Row, Mr, father of, 34, 71

Salter, William, vet, 27, 28, 42, 44, 45, 46, 76

Sandes, Elizabeth, 124

Sandes, Judith, 123, 124

Sandes, Sarah, 123

Sandes, Thomas, 123

Sardgerson and Smith, bill of Anne Morice, 62

Saunders, Mr, 12-13, 36, 37, 47, appeal against Land tax, 72, at Poor rate hearing, 52, 53, painting at the Grove, 69, 71, paying poor rate, 42, stable dampness, 39

Scala, Dr Libovio, 145

Seegar, William, Sexton at Wandsworth, 69

Serman, Catherine, bill, 66, 68

Servants at Naples, bequest, 144

Settlement Act, 58

Shareman, Abraham, see Sherman

Shaw, Henry, agent for Morice, 112

Sherman, Abraham, waterman, 29, 34, 35, 38, death, 37

Shermas, Abraham, see Sherman

Shipway, Lt. Col. Robert, tenant and owner of the Grove, 121

Sich, John, Church rate collector, 55

Silver, coach horse, 21, 23, 36, 48

Slamekin's filly, horse, 21

Slocumb, Charles, 25, 37, 38, 40

Small, beer, 24

Small Pox Hospital, 95, bequest, 132

Smiler, coach horse, 40, 43, 66

Smithfield, market, 40

Snap, dog, 21

South Milton, Devon, 135

Spaven, in horses, 73, 75

Spiers, Mr, letter from, 74, 75

Spring, cold in 1784, 56, 58

Spritely, carthorse, 21, 36, 40

St Georges hospital, 61

Stable hands, see Carter, Robert; Collett, Thom; Cross, Henry; Gould, William; Hankins, John; Pitt, William; Slocumb, Charles; Weeden, John

Stable staff, dates of year end, 62-63, wages, 52

Stacey, see Stracey

Staff year, 62-63, 64

Staff, at the Grove, 17

Staff, size of at the Grove, 9

Staff in Italy, 9

Stamp Office, horse tax, 73, 74

Starke, Susan, 13, 14, 43, bequest, 136, 137, illness, 40, 51

Steers opodeldoc, 43, 46, 61, 63

Stifle, in horse, 59, 60

Stoddiscombe, Devon, 135

Stone, Thomas, witness to Morice's will, 142

Stracey, Thomas, servant, 15, 22, 74, bequest, 135, 137

Strachey, see Stracey

Strand on the Green, 32, 79

Strangles, in horses, 33, 35

Sultan, old coach horse, 43, 48, 51

Surveyors of the Highways, request for money, 55, 76, 78

Susan, see Starke, Susan

Sutcombe, Devon, 135

Sutton Court, staff size, 9

Tack, horse, 21

Tanner Elizabeth, 11, 56, 63, 87

Tanner, old, 87

Tartar, horse, 21, 23, 28, 33, death, 35,

Taxes, local, 16

Taylor Nicholas, cooper, 28, 44

Thompson, Daniel, 66, 67

Tisby, Morice's dog, 70, 71

Tithes, 40, 76, 78

Toper, dog, 21

Toss, dog, 83

Towneley, John, 49, 50, 94

Tremells, Roger, coal dealer, 36, 38, 49, 62

Trethew, Cornwall, 135

Trimells, see Tremells

Truelad, dog, death, 83

Turnham Green, 32, 33, 59, picture of in about 1790, illustration 11*

Twickenham, 35

Twister, dog, 21, 23, 43

Tylney, Lord, 85, 86, 143

Typhus, 77, 78

Upper Ossory, Earl and Countess of, 95

Vaughan, John, gardener, 11, 32, 37, 62, 65, draft of money to, 65, income from walnuts and chestnuts, 73, tubs for orange trees, 54, wage, 17

Venereal disease, 28

Vestry meeting, 35

Vickers, Joseph, porter, 12, 17, 29, 60, fights off burglary attempt, 65, sent to London, 79, wage not paid, 82

Wages, at the Grove, 17, 72-73, 74

Walnuts and chestnuts, sale of, 37, 38, 73, 75, 116

Walnuts, theft, 32

Walpole, Horace, 92

Wandsworth Hill graveyard, 69, 100, 129

Wandsworth, poor of the parish, annuity, 76, bequest to, 132

Wapshot, William, butcher, bill for dog meat, 27, 29, 66, 67, 84, 86, draft for, 86, request for House and Window tax, 55, 76, 78

Watson, Richard, 125

Weatherly, owner of lodgings, 84

Weatherstone, Mr, 33, 35

Webb, Joseph, witness to Naples will, 144

Weeden, John, stable hand, 10, annual wage, date of year end, 62, 82, illness, 11, 28, 61, 63, money received, 52, needs new boots, 67, new clothes, 37

Werrington, , 10, 22, 43, 46, 80, 81, 86, 91, 92, picture, illustration 4*

Wheat straw, 33, 37

White, Mrs Jane, bequest, 143

Whitefoot, carthorse, not well, 85

Whyddon, Devon, 135

Wills, Thomas, 84, 86

Wilmot, Mr, solicitor, 16, 143

Window tax, 55, 57, 76, 78

Wingood, Elizabeth, old servant, 43, 45, bequest, 136, 137

Winter, cold, (1784), 47, 50

Wood, John atte, 111

Wood John, 10, illness, 51, 53

Wood Walton, Huntingdon, 99, 130, poor of the parish, bequest, 132

Workhouse, Chiswick, 84, 86

Wright, Matthew, bricklayer, 28, 31, 76

Youd, Charles, witness to Morice's will, 142